THE CIVIL WAR

IN

500

PHOTOGRAPHS

TOP LEFT AND RIGHT: Soldiers, Union and Confederate, adjusted to camp life. MIDDLE: Drill was part of the troops' daily existence. BOTTOM: General Grant, on the far left, photographed with staff following the Union victory at Lookout Mountain, outside Chattanooga, Tennessee, in 1963

CONTENTS

Political and social differences between the North and South steadily increased from the 1830s on. The issues of slavery, states' rights, and tariffs on foreign goods created a rift between the industrial North and agricultural South.

A new nation was born as the Confederate States of America assembled. President Abraham Lincoln prepared to go war to preserve the Union, while Southerners took up arms to defend their way of life.

All across the country, men joined military service in droves. While the Union and Confederate causes were at odds, the soldiers themselves were more alike than they were different.

The second year of the war brought carnage that shocked the country, North and South. Ulysses S. Grant rose through the ranks of the Union army and Robert E. Lee took command of the Army of Northern Virginia.

Naval operations during the Civil War ushered in significant leaps in technology. Northern industry boomed as it built the Federal armada, while Southern innovation modernized naval warfare on a shoestring.

The Emancipation Proclamation reconfigured the war into a fight against slavery. Confederate forces moved to attack the North, and the two armies clashed in a fierce three-day battle at Gettysburg.

As war raged on, civilian life was dramatically affected, particularly in the South. In many places, women were left to run plantations and farms and cared for the young and old alike.

Northern forces closed in on the South. Naval blockades cut off a vital lifeline and the Confederate economy crumbled. The end of the war was in sight.

Southern forces surrendered and the Thirteenth Amendment ended slavery in America. Following Lincoln's assassination the country moves to mend its considerable wounds.

Introduction

Perhaps more than any other conflict in the history of the United States of America, the Civil War changed the course of the country. The expansive growth during the first 90 years of the Union ushered in great change, especially in the Northern states where metropolises were forming and industry was taking off. The Southern states, largely agricultural with cotton and tobacco plantations fueled by slave labor, were slower to transform. The early American ideals of small government and the individual rights of the states remained strong in the region. The divide between the two ways of life became insurmountable, and in 1861, America went to war with itself.

The fight to preserve the Union transformed into a war against slavery, and when it was over, America emerged an altered nation. During the four years of the conflict, 620,000 lives were lost, whole towns and cities burned, and virtually no American was left unaffected. *The Civil War in 500 Photographs* chronicles this heart-wrenching and heroic narrative, while serving as a record of the emerging capabilities of the photographer's lens.

The new technology of photography was rapidly developing at the time, and as the conflict intensified, photojournalism and battlefield photography took hold, thanks to pioneers like Mathew Brady and George S. Cook.

Today, the pictures, while over 150 years old, have lost none of their power to communicate the brutality of war. Readers will note that while the photographs of the era were black and white or sepia-toned, *The Civil War in 500 Photographs* contains some images that have been colorized, providing a new sense of urgency to the stories they tell. The stoicism of troops assembled for battle and the determination of generals plotting strategies draw the viewer in, while the fields of dead and wounded offer irrefutable reminders of the incredible cost of this conflict.

In the words of Abraham Lincoln: "The mystic chords of memory, stretching from every battlefield and patriot grave to every living heart and hearthstone all over this broad land, will yet swell the chorus of the Union, when again touched, as surely they will be, by the better angels of our nature." This collection pulls at the same mystic chord—the one that connects brother to brother and all Americans across the nation.

A Union soldier from the 8th Pennsylvania Infantry held the tattered flag of his division with pride.

1 A GROWING FISSURE

IN THE DECADES LEADING TO THE CIVIL WAR, THE NORTH AND THE SOUTH STEADILY DRIFTED APART. BY 1860, THE UNITED STATES HAD IN MANY WAYS BECOME TWO NATIONS WITHIN ONE.

The United States capitol as it appeared in 1846. In the decades leading up to the Civil War, America's political leaders struggled to mend the widening breach between the North and the South.

"A house divided against itself cannot stand."

—Abraham Lincoln, June 16, 1858

In 1860, New York was the most populous city in America. Broadway bustled with activity.

Demand for American cotton soared in 1860. Increasing exports to the Northern states and Britain boosted production and greatly increased the value of slaves on Southern cotton plantations.

America in 1860: High Hopes and a Widening Divide

IN SPITE OF NATIONAL ECONOMIC GROWTH, CULTURAL AND POLITICAL DIFFERENCES SEPARATED THE NORTH AND SOUTH.

In 1860, the United States was a youthful, vibrant, and rapidly growing nation. Only 84 years had passed since the founding fathers crafted the Declaration of Independence, yet in that time, America had become a vast nation that sprawled across the entire continent. The population had swelled from less than 4 million to more than 31 million, thanks largely to immigration. Although increasing numbers of Americans were taking up urban trades, most were still farmers, especially in the South and the Western territories.

The economy enjoyed steady growth too, fueled by a parade of recent inventions including the sewing machine, the electric locomotive, the hydraulic turbine, the Bessemer steel process, and the Otis elevator. A golden age of shipbuilding enabled the United States to produce almost as much tonnage as Great Britain and all its colonies combined. Major cities such as New York—which boasted more than 800,000 residents in 1860—emerged from an era where pigs wandered dirt streets to an era of horse-drawn streetcars, paved streets, and city waterworks systems.

In the single decade of the 1850s, the amount of railroad track in the United States increased from approximately 9,000 miles to more than 30,000. Americans were eyewitnesses to a nation on the move, if not participants in it.

And yet, a cultural and political chasm was widening across the country, and no one seemed able to heal it. Soon, that chasm would claim the lives of more than 620,000 Americans.

UNITED STATES IN 1860

The U.S. government regulated the spread of slavery into Western Territories through a series of legislation shown here.

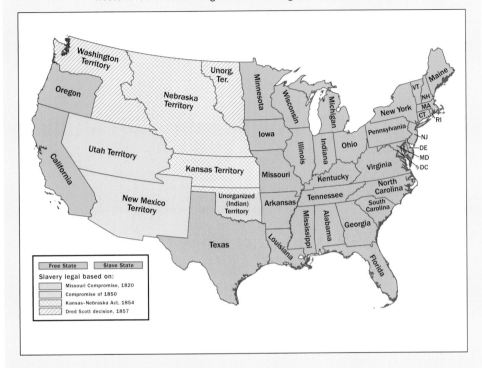

Free State | Slave State
Slavery legal based on:
Missouri Compromise, 1820
Compromise of 1850
Kansas–Nebraska Act, 1854
Dred Scott decision, 1857

Steamboats lined the levee along the Mississippi River in St. Louis.

KEEPING COUNT

THE LARGEST AMERICAN CITIES IN 1860

The 1860 U.S. Census ranked these as the top ten cities in the United States, according to population. Seven were located in the North; Baltimore and St. Louis were in border states. Only New Orleans was in the South.

1. NEW YORK, NY
805,651

2. PHILADELPHIA, PA
562,529

3. BROOKLYN, NY
266,661

4. BALTIMORE, MD
212,418

5. BOSTON, MA
177,812

6. NEW ORLEANS, LA
168,675

7. CINCINNATI, OH
161,044

8. ST. LOUIS, MO
160,773

9. CHICAGO, IL
109,260

10. BUFFALO, NY
81,129

Manufacturing and government-supported works projects, along with the development of the railroad system, fueled an economic boom in Northern cities. Railroad expansion proved particularly vital to the war effort on both sides of the conflict.

In the prewar years, the South remained an agrarian culture, as its agricultural production—most notably of cotton—was extremely profitable and precluded the need for significant industrial expansion.

Two Nations in One: North vs. South

DISAGREEMENTS ON ISSUES LIKE IMPORT TARIFFS AND THE ROLE OF THE CENTRAL GOVERNMENT DROVE A DEEP WEDGE BETWEEN INDUSTRIAL AND AGRARIAN AREAS.

Despite having much in common, Northerners and Southerners had drifted apart because of politics, but also because the regions had two distinctively different cultures. The South was an agricultural society, controlled by the owners of large plantations. Southerners, generally traditional and conservative, were suspicious of a large national government. They favored states' rights and opposed taxation on imported goods. The South grew almost all of the nation's cotton, produced a majority of the country's military leaders, and had provided 9 of the first 15 American presidents.

The North, in contrast, was increasingly urban, progressive, and industrial. It held almost 90 percent of the nation's manufacturing, most of its railroads, and two-thirds of its population. The region's political leaders generally favored tariffs on imports to protect Northern business and industry, championed government-supported projects, and advocated a strong national government.

Fuel on the Smoldering Fire

The North's push for higher tariffs on imports incensed Southerners, who imported most manufactured items and feared higher prices.

They believed that Northern leaders, if unchecked, would eventually rule not only the states, but also the daily lives of individual Americans. In turn, many Northerners saw Southern politicians as demanding, obstructionist, unpatriotic, and self-serving.

The issue of slavery was like fuel tossed on a smoldering fire of sectional rivalry. As Northern criticism of slavery increased, Southerners felt condemned and a nationalist movement steadily emerged. Many were alarmed when Northern newspapers hailed abolitionist John Brown as a hero for attempting to launch a slave revolt at Harpers Ferry, West Virginia, in 1859. Their sense of isolation deepened further the next year when Abraham Lincoln and the fledgling Republican Party—both of which were viewed as anti-Southern and antislavery—carried the presidential election.

A Divisive National Issue

In the United States, there was little consensus on the slavery question from the time the first Africans were brought ashore in 1619 to the day South Carolina seceded in 1860.

1619 Slavery introduced to America in the colony of Virginia.

1787 Northwest Ordinance enacted by Congress restricted slavery in Northern territories.

1793 First Fugitive Slave Act required return of escaped slaves.

1794 Eli Whitney's cotton gin spurred demand for slave labor.

1807: Congress outlawed the importation of slaves from abroad.

1831 Nat Turner slave revolt in Virginia alarmed Southerners.

1852 *Uncle Tom's Cabin* by Harriet Beecher Stowe was published.

1855 Violent attacks in Kansas occurred as antislavery factions and proslavery raiders clashed.

1856 The newly formed, antislavery Republican Party held its first presidential-nominating convention in Philadelphia.

1857 *Dred Scott* decision by U.S. Supreme Court upheld constitutionality of slavery.

1859 John Brown led an unsuccessful abolitionist raid on U.S. Armory and Arsenal at Harpers Ferry.

1860 Republican Abraham Lincoln elected president; South Carolina seceded from the Union.

ABRAHAM LINCOLN,
REPUBLICAN CANDIDATE FOR PRESIDENT OF THE UNITED STATES

1619

1787

1807

1852

1860

Slave owners often split up families. In spite of this practice, slaves forged strong family ties, and strangers stepped in to care for children separated from their blood relatives.

Slavery Comes to America

SOUTHERN AGRICULTURE HINGED
ON THE SLAVE WORKFORCE.

ROBERT PURVIS
1810–1898

Robert Purvis was a leading American antislavery advocate during the antebellum era. Born in Charleston, South Carolina to a Jewish businessman and a free black woman, he and abolitionist William Lloyd Garrison, publisher of *The Liberator* newspaper, were influential in establishing the American Anti-Slavery Society in Philadelphia in 1833.

The first African slaves in America were brought to Virginia's Jamestown Colony in 1619 aboard an English ship sailing under a Dutch flag. There were approximately 20 of them.

In the decades that followed, America's slave population expanded dramatically and slavery became a national institution that was both allowed by the U.S. Constitution and endorsed in rulings by the U.S. Supreme Court. The North, with its shipping centers like Newport, Rhode Island, served as the slave trade's commercial heart until 1808, when

Congress banned the importation of slaves. Slavery, however, remained legal in many states. In the North, the practice was allowed in New York until 1827, and in New Jersey until 1846, then eventually began to fade.

Not so in the agricultural South where slave labor was considered critical to the region's economy. In 1793, the invention of the cotton gin boosted the crop's profitability and increased the demand for slave labor to produce it. By 1860, most of the 4 million slaves in the United States were held in the Southern states.

As the institution grew, however, so did opposition to it. An increasing number of Americans, including some in the South, believed the institution was harmful to slave owners as well as to slaves. "In the order of divine Providence, the man who puts one end of a chain around the ankle of his fellow man will find the other end around his own neck," said Frederick Douglass, the leading nineteenth century African-American opponent of slavery.

Stoking Southern Fears

While some Southerners wished to see slavery abolished, most slave owners did not, so the abolitionist movement drew its strength from the North. There, public sentiment against slavery gradually increased. By midcentury, Northern abolitionism had become a significant political force, and public criticism of slavery and Southern slave holders had acquired a harsh tone. Meanwhile, unsuccessful slave uprisings, such as Nat Turner's revolt in Virginia in 1832, stoked Southern fears that Northerners were stirring discontent. In response, Southerners became increasingly defensive and viewed those who were antislavery to also be anti-Southern.

SARAH GRIMKE
1792–1873
ANGELINA GRIMKE
1805–1879

Southern sisters fight slavery.

Raised in a prominent family in Charleston, South Carolina, Sarah Grimke, top, and her sister Angelina, bottom, were leading Southern abolitionists in the antebellum era. They eventually moved to Philadelphia, where their views were more acceptable. During the 1830s, the Grimkes became the most popular antislavery speakers.

During the colonial period, slavery was banned in Georgia. However, by the late 18th century, slaves were crucial to Georgia's economy, cultivating vast amounts of rice and cotton.

Before slaves were put on the auction block, they were held in pens like these in Alexandria, Virginia. The city flourished as an auction center due to its location on the railroad and Potomac River.

On plantations, slaves were packed into clusters of poorly constructed, largely unfurnished cabins with dirt floors. In an attempt to appease abolitionists, some slave owners built better housing, raising cabins off the ground and providing slaves with more space.

UNCLE TOM'S CABIN
A novel changes public perception.

As tensions between North and South reached a fever pitch, a novel by abolitionist Harriet Beecher Stowe stoked the sectional rivalry.

Published in 1852, *Uncle Tom's Cabin* sympathetically depicted the plight of American slaves. It sold more than 300,000 copies and inspired countless Northerners to adopt the antislavery position. Many Southerners, however, believed the North also shared the responsibility for slavery and felt unfairly attacked by Stowe's powerful prose.

LEFT: Laws in the South condoned and often required violence perpetrated against slaves. Slave owners could be fined and risked forfeiting their slaves for not punishing them enough. RIGHT: Slaves were sold to the highest bidder at auction houses like this one in Atlanta. During these events, men were often inspected and then sold first, followed by women and children—a process that broke apart families.

Built to house large numbers of people, slave pens in Alexandria, Virginia, were larger than those elsewhere in the South. This complex featured a tailor to clothe slaves before auction, as well as an infirmary to help ensure slaves were healthy enough to fetch high prices.

Sexual abuse of slaves was pervasive, and slave owners were protected under the law. Slaves were also forced to reproduce, either with each other or with their male owners.

Frederick Douglass wrote three autobiographies, classics in American literature, and served, on two occasions, as an advisor to President Lincoln.

THE UNDERGROUND RAILROAD

In the decades leading to the Civil War, untold numbers of slaves escaped to the North and Canada through the Underground Railroad.

This loosely organized system provided temporary shelter and transportation for escaped slaves through Northern states to Canada.

While white Northerners managed the railroad, it was the fortitude of escaped slaves that made it successful. Escaped slave and renowned abolitionist Frederick Douglass made his way north through the Underground Railroad in 1838. Harriett Tubman was a Maryland field hand who took the railroad to freedom in 1849, and helped as many as three hundred slaves escape in the following years. At its peak, the Underground Railroad enabled as many as two thousand slaves a year to escape bondage.

In addition to her work on the Underground Railroad, Harriet Tubman was also a nurse, scout, and spy for the Union army.

As the U.S. Capitol was expanded to accommodate senators and representatives from newly added states, the dome was rebuilt to suit the building's new dimensions. Construction began in 1856.

Congress Fails to Find a Lasting Compromise between Northern and Southern Ideals

LEGISLATORS HAMMERED OUT DEALS ON SLAVERY, BUT BITTER RHETORIC ON CAPITOL HILL WIDENED THE BREACH BETWEEN NORTH AND SOUTH.

JOHN C. CALHOUN
1782–1850

South Carolinian John C. Calhoun served as a U.S. congressman, a U.S. senator, the U.S. secretary of war, the U.S. secretary of state, and as vice president of the United States under Presidents John Quincy Adams and Andrew Jackson. The Yale-educated Calhoun became a leading Southern defender of state's rights and slavery during the decades leading to the Civil War.

As the North and the South competed for control of the nation, the U. S. Congress became the conflict's chief battleground. To promote their vision of a progressive, industrial society, Northern representatives pushed for a federal government that would support canals, national highways, and railroads. Southern lawmakers resisted, defending state sovereignty and promoting an agricultural society. Increasingly, the issue of slavery came to define the differences in the two regions.

As the nation expanded westward, both sides fought to make slavery legal or illegal in the new states. The 1820 Missouri Compromise admitted Maine as a free state and Missouri as a slave state. The Compromise of 1850 admitted California as a free state and abolished the slave trade in the nation's capital, while requiring escaped slaves to be returned to their owners. The Kansas-Nebraska Act of 1854 allowed residents of those two territories to decide whether they wanted their territory to be slave or free. The deals delayed but did not resolve the disagreements over slavery and the bitter public rhetoric in Congress widened the breach between North and South.

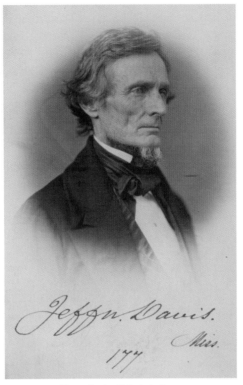

Debate became so heated over the admission of California as a free state that Mississippi senator Henry S. Foote, above, threatened to shoot Senator Thomas Hart Benton of Missouri.

U.S. senator Jefferson Davis of Mississippi emerged as an ardent supporter of both the South and the Union.

TARIFF OF ABOMINATIONS

The last straw for the South

In the early 1800s, tariffs—taxes on imported foreign goods—became a core conflict between the North and South. Northerners favored tariffs to protect American business and industry, most of which were located in the North. The agricultural South imported many manufactured items, and resented Northern leaders pushing for tariffs that raised prices for Southerners.

The most controversial was the Tariff of Abominations, a tax on foreign goods passed in 1828 that drastically raised the cost of living in the Southern states. The tariff was declared invalid in South Carolina where elected officials said it violated the Constitution. The standoff that followed—called the Nullification Crisis—sowed the seeds of a secession movement in South Carolina thirty years before the Civil War.

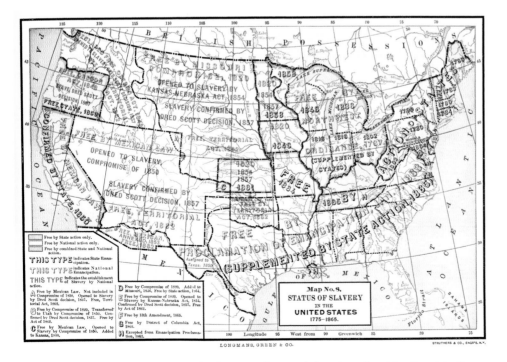

Control of the House of Representatives was held by free states, whose population outgrew slave states. Slave states then needed to control the Senate in order to maintain a veto over federal law. Through a series of complicated compromises, balance was maintained until 1850.

Tensions between antislavery settlers, like those pictured above, and proslavery factions resulted in election fraud and violence as both sides worked to intimidate the other.

Bleeding Kansas

POLITICAL MANEUVERING IN CONGRESS LED
TO VIOLENT CLASHES OF PROSLAVERY AND
ANTISLAVERY FACTIONS IN THE NEW TERRITORY.

In 1854, Northern and Southern political leaders were at odds about how to build a transcontinental railroad. A majority in Congress agreed that the federal government should promote the project by selling public land to railroad companies, but Northern leaders wanted a northern route and Southerners wanted a southern route.

Illinois senator Stephen A. Douglas, a leading Democrat, proposed a central route starting in Chicago. To obtain Southern support in Congress, Douglas authored the 1854 Kansas-Nebraska Act, which allowed residents of those territories to vote on whether they wanted the state to become slave or free.

It was a formula for disaster. Proslavery and antislavery factions sent hordes of settlers into Kansas to determine the voting outcome, and the two sides clashed violently. In 1856, proslavery raiders sacked the free-state town of Lawrence, Kansas, wrecking newspaper offices and burning buildings.

A Nighttime Raid in Kansas

Vowing to "strike terror in the hearts of the proslavery people," John Brown, a militant abolitionist, retaliated three days later with a nighttime raid against Southern families on Pottawatomie Creek in Kansas. Using surplus artillery swords, Brown and his sons dragged five men and boys from their homes, then killed and dismembered them. It turned out that the victims owned no slaves and the murders sparked outrage in the South. The ensuing violence made compromise between the North and South seem impossible.

Democratic senator Stephen A. Douglas sought Southern backing for a central rail route in exchange for his support of slavery in the Kansas territories.

DANIEL WEBSTER
1782–1852

Daniel Webster was an outstanding Constitutional lawyer and served as the U.S. Secretary of State. He also represented Massachusetts in the U.S. Senate. Despite working doggedly with Southern colleagues John C. Calhoun and Henry Clay to avoid a North-South conflict, Webster remained unwavering in his support of the Union. He is remembered for his famous quotation, "Liberty and Union, now and forever, one and inseparable!"

Militant abolitionist John Brown and his sons killed five men from Kansas, sparking outrage in the South.

HENRY CLAY
1777–1852

In the decades leading up to the Civil War, few in Congress worked harder to solve the conflicts between North and South than congressional leader Henry Clay of Kentucky. Although Clay's efforts in the U.S. House and Senate eventually proved futile, he is remembered as the "Great Compromiser" because of his tireless attempts to avoid war between the North and South.

An illustration depicting John Brown's capture at Harpers Ferry. After the episode, he was tried, convicted of treason, and sentenced to death.

John Brown Strikes at Harpers Ferry

AN ATTEMPT TO ROUSE A SLAVE REBELLION IN WEST VIRGINIA ENDED IN A STANDOFF BETWEEN MILITANT ABOLITIONISTS AND THE U.S. ARMY.

On a Sunday evening in autumn 1859, militant abolitionist John Brown reappeared on the public stage. Leading an 18-man armed gang, he attempted to seize the U.S. Armory and Arsenal at Harpers Ferry, Virginia in order to arm a slave insurrection and set up an antislavery republic in the Appalachians.

The attack was a fiasco. The first man killed was a free black worker who got in the gang's way and Brown himself was soon wounded. As the hours wore on, the raiders took a group of hostages and retreated to a nearby fire station. It took a contingent of U.S. Marines, lead by Robert E. Lee—then a colonel in the U.S. Army—to restore order and arrest the raiders.

Eventually Brown was tried and convicted of treason. On November 2, 1859, he was hauled to the gallows in a wagon, seated on his coffin. The events put Southerners on edge, especially when it was revealed that the raid had been funded by a half-dozen Northern businessmen.

Southern anger spilled into outrage when prominent Northerners publicly declared Brown as a martyr and compared him to Jesus Christ. Passion seemed to overtake caution in both the North and the South.

Antislavery fanatic John Brown, as he appeared in 1859.

Brown and his raiders barricaded themselves and their hostages in this brick firehouse.

At the time of the Harpers Ferry Raid, Colonel Robert E. Lee was at his home in Arlington, Virginia, on leave from command of the U.S. 2nd Cavalry in Texas. He was ordered by his superiors to round up a contingent of U.S. Marines, take them to Harpers Ferry, and end the raid.

The view of the armory at Harpers Ferry from the river side.

Dred Scott was a Missouri slave who sued for his freedom. The case worked its way to the U.S. Supreme Court, which ruled in support of slavery.

In the *Dred Scott* case, U.S. Supreme Court chief justice Roger B. Taney wrote that black Americans, slave or free, "had no rights which the white man was bound to respect."

Harsh Words and Court Action Fuel the Fires

LEGISLATION FURTHER DIVIDED THE
COUNTRY ON THE ISSUE OF SLAVERY.

By 1860, the distrust between the North and the South was nearing a climax, fueled by recurring controversy and heated public rhetoric.

The Fugitive Slave Act of 1850 infuriated many Northerners by requiring local law enforcement officials to return escaped slaves. Southern leaders were angered when some Northern states defied federal law and refused. In the 1857 *Dred Scott* case, the U.S. Supreme Court ruled that slavery was constitutional, could not be barred from the Western territories, and that persons of African descent could not become American citizens. Amid the controversies, Northern and Southern newspapers stirred emotions with angry editorials.

The tempers in Washington ran equally hot. As Congress struggled to find compromises over slavery and other issues between the North and the South, fiery rhetoric from both sides fueled passions and further pushed the factions apart. Northern congressman Thaddeus Stevens denounced a proslavery Democrat as a "skunk" on the floor of Congress, and accused Southerners of "tyranny" and "treason." After Massachusetts senator Charles Sumner harshly criticized South Carolina senator Andrew Butler, Congressman Preston Brooks—a relative of Butler's—beat Sumner almost senseless with a cane on the floor of the Senate. Southern business leader Isaac Trimble likewise denounced the North: "Our connection with you never had, from the early settlement of the colonies 'til now, any bond but that of political interest. Your bigotry & hatred of everything Southern drove us from you. . . ."

On the floor of the U.S. senate, Massachusetts senator Charles Sumner vilified Senator Stephen Douglas as "an animal" and accused South Carolina senator Andrew Butler of committing adultery with "the harlot slavery."

After beating Senator Charles Sumner with a cane, Congressman Preston Brooks resigned his seat in the House of Representatives, but he was re-elected by the people of South Carolina who supported his act of violence.

A newspaper illustration depicted Brooks pounding Sumner with a cane on the floor of the U.S. Senate. Brooks became a hero in the South and Sumner became a martyr in the North.

Northern Democrat Stephen Douglas consistently advocated for a middle ground in the debate on slavery, believing in the principle of popular sovereignty.

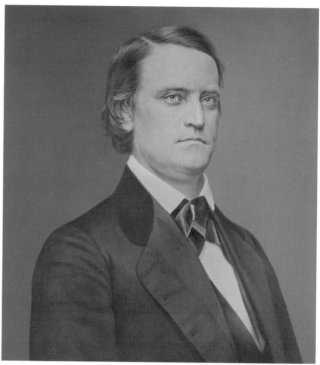

Southern Democrat John C. Breckinridge ran for the presidency on a proslavery platform. After the start of the war, he encouraged his home state of Kentucky to secede from the Union before he fled south.

Constitutional Union Party candidate John Bell won support from the border states with his temperate stance on slavery and antisecessionist views.

Republican candidate Abraham Lincoln asserted that slavery was in direct opposition to the values of the founding fathers as stated in the Declaration of Independence.

The North Triumphs in the 1860 Election

THE REPUBLICAN VICTORIES BOLSTERED THE ANTISLAVERY CAUSE AND IGNITED THE SOUTH TO ACTION.

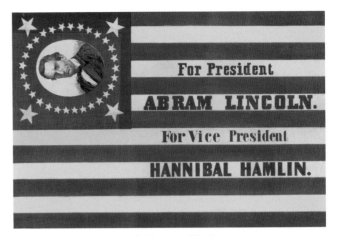

A Republican campaign banner for Lincoln and Hamlin.

As the 1860 presidential contest approached, America was bitterly divided. All the issues that had provoked conflict between the North and the South were now points of contention in the election—the role of the federal government, states' rights, tariffs, the route of a transcontinental railroad, and, especially, slavery. The Democratic Party split under the pressure: Northern Democrats nominated proslavery Senator Stephen Douglas, while the Southern wing nominated its own proslavery candidate, John C. Breckinridge, who was vice president at the time. The hastily formed and short-lived Constitutional Union Party, composed mainly of members of the collapsed Whig Party, put forth U.S. senator John Bell of Tennessee.

After prolonged convention banter, the fledgling Republican Party nominated Abraham Lincoln, viewed as a compromise candidate. Lincoln opposed slavery, but was content to restrict it to existing slave states rather than abolish it everywhere. With so many choices, no candidate won a majority of the popular vote. Lincoln received less than 40 percent—a plurality—but he won a solid majority of 180 electoral votes, making him the first Republican president of the United States.

Southerners were disheartened. The winning party's opposition to slavery as well as its support for tariffs and a strong federal government, meant the 1860 election was a triumph for the North and a disaster for the South.

Senator Hannibal Hamlin of Maine was chosen as Abraham Lincoln's running mate.

THE LINCOLN-DOUGLAS DEBATES

When Illinois senator Stephen A. Douglas ran for reelection in 1858, he faced a formidable opponent in Abraham Lincoln, a former state legislator and one-term congressman who opposed the Kansas-Nebraska Act.

The two engaged in a series of seven debates, with slavery as the chief topic. While Douglas favored the practice, Lincoln's position was more nuanced. He denounced slavery but was also willing to allow it to continue in the existing slave states, and favored freeing the slaves over the course of about forty years through "gradual emancipation." Douglas, who was better known and more influential, won the race. Lincoln, however, also profited. The debates made him a national figure and positioned him for the Republican presidential nomination in 1860.

The Union is Dissolved

SOUTH CAROLINA SECEDED FROM THE UNITED STATES
OF AMERICA AND TIPPED THE SCALES TO WAR.

A s results from the presidential election of
November 6, 1860 rolled in, the state legislature
met in Charleston and remained in session for the
day. When the news of Lincoln's victory arrived,
the lawmakers voted to convene an emergency
state election.

On December 20, 1860, the delegates met in
Charleston and unanimously voted for the ordinance
of secession, declaring South Carolina to be an
independent republic and no longer a part of the
United States of America. Some South Carolinians
received the news with despair; most, however,
welcomed secession with joyful celebration.

ABOVE: The South Carolina Secession Convention
RIGHT: Charleston's Institute Hall where South Carolina delegates
signed the Ordinance of Secession declaring the state no longer
part of the United States of America.

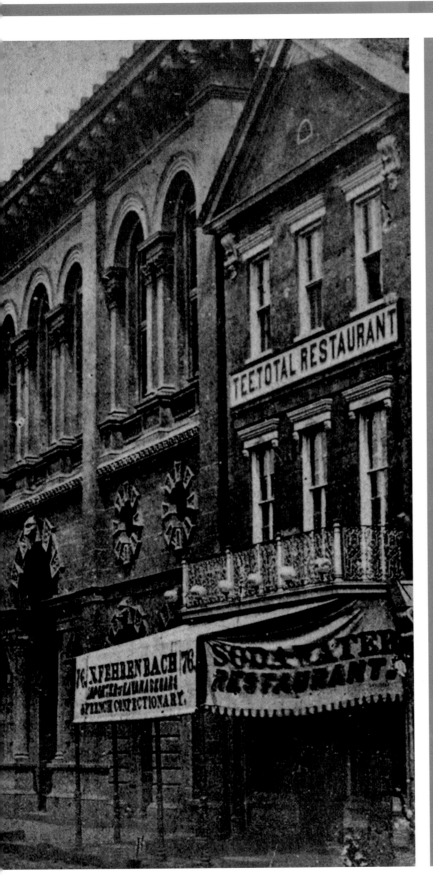

A SPECIAL EDITION

When South Carolina's secession convention voted to take the Palmetto State out of the Union, the staff at the *Charleston Mercury* was standing by their printing press to report the news. Fifteen minutes after the monumental vote, the 35-year-old newspaper was ready to distribute a special edition broadside topped by a giant headline: "The Union is Dissolved."

On the street outside the newspaper office, the paper was read to a crowd of Charlestonians, which erupted in cheers. The text of the *Mercury's* special edition:

Passed unanimously at 1.15 o'clock, P.M., December 20th, 1860. An ordinance to dissolve the Union between the State of South Carolina and other States united with her under the compact entitled "The Constitution of the United States of America."

We, the People of the State of South Carolina, in Convention assembled, do declare and ordain, and it is hereby declared and ordained,

That the Ordinance adopted by us in Convention, on the twenty-third day of May, in the year of our Lord one thousand seven hundred and eighty-eight, whereby the Constitution of the United States of America was ratified, and also, all Acts and parts of Acts of the General Assembly of this State, ratifying amendments of the said Constitution, are hereby repealed; and that the union now subsisting between South Carolina and other States, under the name of "The United States of America," is hereby dissolved. The Union is dissolved.

Secessionists celebrated in Charleston.

2

1861: BROTHER AGAINST BROTHER

THE DECADES OF TENSION AND SECTIONAL RIVALRY BETWEEN THE NORTH AND THE SOUTH REACHED A BOILING POINT. IN 1861, AMERICA WENT TO WAR WITH ITSELF.

Northern troops assembled for drill at Fort Richardson, a new fortification built to defend Washington, D.C. in 1861.

"[Warfare] might have been avoided, if forbearance and wisdom had been practiced on both sides."

—Confederate general Robert E. Lee, February 17, 1866

Confederate president Jefferson Davis and his new cabinet were depicted in a lithograph assembling in Montgomery, Alabama in 1861.

JUDAH P. BENJAMIN
1811-1884

In 1861, the Confederate congress appointed South Carolinian Judah P. Benjamin as Attorney General of the Confederacy—the first Jewish American cabinet member. He also served as the C.S. Secretary of State, and was President Davis's closest friend and advisor. After the war he became a prominent attorney in Britain.

The Dawn of the Confederate States of America

SOUTHERNERS CONVENED IN MONTGOMERY, ALABAMA ELECTED TO FORM A NEW NATION AND ELECTED A NEW COMMANDER IN CHIEF.

In the six weeks that followed South Carolina's secession, a half dozen more Southern states voted to leave the Union: Mississippi, Florida, Alabama, Georgia, Louisiana, and Texas. By February, the seven states had agreed to send delegates to a meeting in Montgomery, Alabama to form a new government, and within days, attendees declared they had formed a provisional congress for a new nation, the Confederate States of America. The Montgomery conventioneers promptly adopted a constitution, chose former U.S. senator Jefferson Davis of Mississippi as president, and former U.S. congressman Alexander Stephens of Georgia as vice president.

Building a Government from Scratch

Tiny Montgomery, the Confederacy's new national capital, was soon jammed with politicians, soldiers, newspaper reporters, lobbyists, and office seekers. "Everybody who comes here wants an office," observed the wife of a former U.S. senator. "And I thought we had left all that in Washington."

In his inauguration speech, seen in this illustration, Confederate president Jefferson Davis stated his hope that "the beginning of our career as a Confederacy may not be obstructed by hostile opposition."

The Confederate government modeled itself on the U.S. government, with a bicameral congress, a judiciary, and an executive branch. The Confederate Constitution resembled the U.S. Constitution, except that it limited the president and vice president to single six-year terms, prohibited tariffs on imports, promoted states' rights, and clearly declared slavery to be legal.

An Overnight Switch

The Confederate congress also established six government departments: treasury, state, justice, war, navy, and post office—with former employees of the U.S. Post Office switching to the C.S. Post Office overnight. To create its first run of national currency, Confederate officials hired an engraving company in New York City. On February 18, 1861 in a ceremony on the front portico of the stately Alabama capitol, Jefferson Davis was inaugurated as the president of the Confederate States of America. A few months later, the Confederate capital was moved to Richmond, Virginia.

1861

The Lead-up to War

The conflict escalated as Southern states seceded and the North took action to preserve the Union.

January 10–February 1 Florida, Alabama, Georgia, Louisiana, and Texas seceded.

February 18 Jefferson Davis inaugurated president of the Confederate States of America.

March 4 Abraham Lincoln inaugurated president of the United States of America.

April 14 Fort Sumter surrendered to Confederate forces.

April 15 President Lincoln called for 75,000 troops to suppress "insurrection."

April 17 Virginia seceded.

April 19 President Lincoln ordered a naval blockade of Southern seaports.

May 6 Arkansas seceded.

May 20 North Carolina seceded.

June 8 Tennessee seceded.

July 21 Battle of First Bull Run—first major land battle of the Civil War.

Jefferson Davis: All We Ask Is to Be Left Alone

A RELUCTANT LEADER, DAVIS SERVED AS THE FIRST AND ONLY PRESIDENT OF THE CONFEDERATE STATES OF AMERICA.

Like Abraham Lincoln, Jefferson Davis was born in central Kentucky in the first decade of the 19th century. There, however, the two men's paths parted. While Lincoln traveled to the North, Davis and his family headed for the deep South. Davis grew up in Mississippi's plantation culture, graduated from West Point, and served as an officer in the U.S. Army.

He married the daughter of future president Zachary Taylor, but she died from an illness soon after their wedding. Davis remarried, to Varina Howell of Natchez, Mississippi, pursued the planter's life, and was elected to U.S. Congress. Davis resigned to command troops in the Mexican War, and became a war hero at the Battle of Buena Vista, which afterward helped him secure a seat from Mississippi in the U.S. Senate. In 1853, President Franklin Pierce appointed him U.S. secretary of war, but Davis returned to the Senate in 1857, rising to become the principal champion of the South, along with John C. Calhoun.

In the Rose Garden

Davis was pruning rose bushes at his Mississippi plantation in February 1861 when a courier arrived with a telegram offering him the presidency of the newly formed Confederate States. He

A presidential portrait of Jefferson Davis

In 1845, Jefferson Davis, a widower, married Varina Howell. At 36, he was considerably older than his 19-year-old bride.

The Brockenbrough home, in Richmond, Virginia, became the Confederate president's official residence when the Confederate capital was moved to the city.

left immediately for Montgomery and his new post. But while he defended the South and slavery, he was a reluctant secessionist. Davis spoke of being president "as a man might speak of a sentence of death," his wife later said.

Davis brought zeal and experience to the job. Like many Northern leaders, he considered himself to be faithful to the ideals of America's founding fathers. In his inauguration speech, Davis called for a peaceful separation from the Union, while sounding a warning to the North: "the courage and patriotism of the people of the Confederate States will be found equal to any measures of defense which honor and security may require."

As the Confederate president, Davis was a gifted leader of high character with a clear vision for the new nation. "All we ask is to be left alone," he implored the North. Davis's military experience, however, hampered his effectiveness as commander in chief. He was criticized for over-managing the affairs of subordinates and accused of being dogmatic and inflexible.

THE STARS AND BARS AND THE STARRY CROSS
A Nod to the Union

During the early months of 1861, the Flag and Seal Committee of the Confederate worked to create a national flag that was red, white, and and blue in a nod to the Union's "Stars and Stripes."

The chosen design, adopted in March, is credited to a Prussian-born Alabama portrait artist named Nichola Marschall. But the banner looked so much like the U.S. flag that it caused confusion on the battlefield and military leaders developed the "Starry Cross" battle flag as an alternative.

Throughout the war, the Confederate congress continued to propose new versions of a national flag. The last one was adopted barely a month before Lee's surrender at Appomattox in 1865.

The first Confederate National Flag: the "Stars and Bars"

The Confederate battle flag: the "Starry Cross"

At age 51, former U.S. congressman Abraham Lincoln of Illinois became the 16th president of the United States presiding over a broken nation.

Abraham Lincoln: An Unlikely President

DESPITE DOUBTS ABOUT HIS ABILITY, LINCOLN ASSUMED LEADERSHIP, UNDETERRED.

"I hold myself . . . the humblest of all individuals that have ever been elevated to the presidency," Abraham Lincoln told supporters while en route to his inauguration at the Capitol in Washington, D.C on March 4, 1861.

Certainly Lincoln had one of the most modest backgrounds of all U.S. presidents. He was born in a crude one-room cabin in Kentucky in 1809, and by age nine had witnessed the deaths of a baby brother and his mother. His father, who remarried, moved the family from one farm to another in Kentucky, Indiana, and Illinois.

Abraham Lincoln gave his first inaugural address on the steps of the Capitol to a crowd of nearly 25,000 people, and security was of the utmost importance. The president-elect had received many death threats—more than 10,000 would come throughout his time as president—and it was known that secessionists sought to impede his inauguration.

The constant uprooting meant Lincoln only received about a year of formal schooling, but he studied history, math, and other subjects on his own.

In 1830, the family moved to New Salem, Illinois, and a year later, at 22, Lincoln set out on his own. He first served a brief stint as a captain of militia in an Indian uprising known as the Black Hawk War, then worked as a storekeeper, a village postmaster, and a road surveyor. Finally, in his late 20s, Lincoln taught himself the law and was licensed to practice in Springfield, the state capital.

Dismissed as a Backwoods Rube

Lincoln prospered as an attorney and over the next twenty years he became one of the highest-paid railroad lawyers in Illinois. He married Kentucky belle Mary Todd, and together they had four sons. In 1846, he was elected to the U.S. Congress. After just one term, Lincoln returned to Illinois, first winning a seat in the state legislature, then quitting to run unsuccessfully for the U.S. Senate as a Republican. That race, against incumbent proslavery Democrat Stephen Douglas, helped Lincoln garner support that would fuel his run for the White House in 1860.

As a presidential candidate, Lincoln was considered a moderate. He was ardently committed to preserving the Union and opposed to slavery, but was willing to allow the practice in the Southern states where it existed. The views, however, did not earn him respect in the eastern political establishment. He was dismissed him as a backwoods rube whose election was a disastrous fluke, and newspapers throughout the North declared him unfit for the presidency.

Undeterred, Lincoln kept his focus on saving the Union. At his inauguration, he urged the Southern states to return to the fold, citing "mystic chords of memory, stretching from every battle-field and patriot grave" that united all Americans. He also issued what many Southerners took as a threat: "I shall take care, as the Constitution itself expressly enjoins upon me, that the laws of the Union shall be faithfully executed in all the States. . . ."

Born into a prominent slave-owning family in Kentucky, Mary Todd was a witty, vivacious Southern belle who met Abraham Lincoln while visiting a sister in Illinois. The two married in 1842.

Based on eyewitness accounts, this 1861 color lithograph by Northern publisher Currier & Ives depicted the bombardment of Fort Sumter.

First Fire on Fort Sumter

ON APRIL 12, 1861 THE CONFEDERATE FORCES ATTACKED A U.S. ARMY POST AND THE CIVIL WAR BEGAN.

At twilight on December 26, 1860, U.S. Army Major Robert Anderson issued a surprise order to the U.S. troops posted to Charleston, South Carolina: Pack up and be ready to move out in 20 minutes. Anderson was the senior U.S. Army officer in Charleston and was alarmed that the Palmetto State had seceded. He wanted to relocate his garrison to the most defensible position under his command: an army post on a small island in the middle of Charleston's harbor known as Fort Sumter.

South Carolina officials viewed Anderson's move as an act of war. Governor Francis Pickens officially asked federal authorities in Washington to withdraw the major and his garrison. Instead, outgoing President James Buchannan dispatched an unarmed ship, the *Star of the West,* to reinforce Fort Sumter. On January 9, 1861—in what was arguably the first shot of the Civil War—the *Star of the West* was turned back by artillery fire from South Carolina troops as it approached Charleston.

A State for a Fort

By the time Lincoln was inaugurated in March, Anderson and his men had prepared for battle and Fort Sumter had become the standoff between the North and the South. Charleston Harbor was ringed with artillery batteries manned by Confederate soldiers. President Davis insisted that no Federal soldiers could remain on Confederate land and even offered to pay to transport Anderson and his men elsewhere. But Lincoln's cabinet was divided on whether to evacuate the fort. The president openly considered a proposal to abandon Fort Sumter if Virginia in exchange would agree to remain in the Union. "A state for a fort is not a bad business," he declared.

Major Robert Anderson, the Northern commander of Fort Sumter, was a former instructor at West Point, where he had taught General Beauregard, the Confederate commander opposing him at Charleston.

Brigadier General P.G.T. Beauregard, the commander of the Southern forces that bombarded Fort Sumter, considered Major Anderson to be a friend.

Major Robert Anderson, seated second from the left in the front row, and the officers who served under him at Fort Sumter

In April of 1861, Fort Sumter was a newly constructed masonry fortification built on a small island in Charleston's harbor. It was named for Revolutionary War hero General Thomas Sumter.

MAJOR ROBERT ANDERSON

1805–1871

As tensions mounted at Fort Sumter, unionists believed that having Major Robert Anderson, a Southerner, hold the fortress would be seen as a conciliatory gesture to the Confederates and stave off an attack. The strategy failed, but even after Anderson surrendered, he was hailed as a hero in North. He went on a tour recruiting soldiers and raising money for the Union cause.

After U.S. Army forces surrendered, the Confederate flag was raised over the fort's burned-out barracks and battered ramparts.

Southern officials examined one of the fort's artillery pieces following the surrender.

Confederate artillery was trained on Charleston Harbor. In the distance, Fort Sumter rose above the harbor waters.

Time to Fight or Back Down?

Complicating the crisis, Lincoln's secretary of state William Henry Seward opened backdoor negotiations with the South using former U.S. Supreme Court Justice John A. Campbell, a Confederate sympathizer, as an intermediary. Seward assured the Southern leaders that Lincoln would abandon Fort Sumter, and Confederate commander General P.G.T. Beauregard opened negotiations with Major Anderson on how to best evacuate the stronghold.

Instead of evacuating Fort Sumter, however, President Lincoln officially notified South Carolina governor Francis Wilkinson Pickens that he was dispatching a military expedition to resupply it.

Confederate leaders felt betrayed. Believing it was time to either fight or back down, President Davis ordered General Beauregard to open fire if Major Anderson refused to surrender. When a Southern delegation brought Anderson the ultimatum, the major explained that he could not surrender without orders. Solemnly, he and the Southerners shook hands and said good-bye. "If we never meet in this world again," Anderson said, "God grant that we may meet in the next."

Opening a Thunderous Attack

At 4:30 AM on April 12, 1861, the Confederate artillery batteries opened a thunderous attack on Fort Sumter. Across the harbor in Charleston, residents watched the bombardment from their rooftops; some wept. Anderson's troops returned fire with Fort Sumter's artillery, but they were outgunned. At 1:00 PM the next day, with the fort barracks ablaze and the fire threatening the nearby powder magazine, Major Anderson agreed to surrender.

Unlike the four-year bloodbath that would follow, no one on either side was killed during the fighting. The conflict's sole death occurred on April 14, during the official surrender ceremony, when Major Anderson's troops were firing a salute to the U.S. flag. A cannon exploded, slaying an Irish-born private named Daniel Hough. He was the first of more than 620,000 Americans who would die in the Civil War.

GENERAL P.G.T. BEAUREGARD

1818–1893

Born on a Louisiana sugar plantation, Pierre Gustave Toutant Beauregard trained as a civil engineer and served in the Mexican-American War under General Winfield Scott. He was the first Confederate brigadier general to be named in the Civil War, though he had tense relationships with his commanding officers and President Jefferson Davis. During the stand off at Fort Sumter, Beauregard sent U.S. Army Major Robert Anderson, his former instructor at West Point, cases of brandy and cigars as a gesture of respect. Anderson refused them.

Mary Boykin Chestnut was among the many Charlestonians who watched the bombardment of Fort Sumter from their rooftops, as depicted in this 1861 newspaper image.

WITNESS TO WAR

The Diary of Mary Chestnut

THE CIVIL WAR'S OPENING COMBAT WAS WITNESSED
FROM A CHARLESTON, SOUTH CAROLINA ROOFTOP

South Carolinian Mary Boykin, above, and her husband James were active in the ruling circles of the Confederate States government. Her wartime journal entries were eventually published as *A Diary from Dixie* and became a classic of Civil War literature.

When Confederate forces opened fire on Fort Sumter, one of the civilians who witnessed it was South Carolinian Mary Boykin Chestnut. The daughter of a South Carolina governor, Mary was married to James Chestnut, Jr., a former U.S. senator from South Carolina who served as an aide to General P.G.T. Beauregard. Although Mary Chestnut personally despised slavery, she was devoted to the South and enthusiastically supported the Confederacy. She began keeping a diary early in the war, and continued it throughout the conflict. Her proximity to key people and events produced an extraordinary eyewitness account of the Civil War, which would be published long after her death as *A Diary from Dixie*. In April of 1861, she observed the bombardment of Fort Sumter from a Charleston rooftop—as reported in this excerpt from her diary:

No sleep for anybody last night. The streets were alive with soldiers, men shouting, marching, singing. . . . Today things seem to have settled down a little. One can but hope still.

Lincoln and Seward have made such silly advances and then far sillier drawings back. There may be a chance for peace, after all. Things are happening so fast. . . . Why did that green goose Anderson go into Fort Sumter? Then everything began to go wrong. . . .

April 12, 1861

I did not pretend to go to sleep. How can I? If Anderson does not accept terms—at four— the orders are—he shall be fired upon. I count four—Saint Michael chimes. I begin to hope. At half-past four, the heaving booming of a cannon.

I sprang out of bed. And on my knees—prostrate—I prayed as I never prayed before.

There was a sound of stir all over the house—pattering of feet in the corridor—all seemed hurrying one way. I put on my double gown and a shawl and went, too. It was to the housetop.

The shells were bursting. In the dark I heard a man say, "waste of ammunition."

I knew my husband was rowing about in a boat somewhere in that dark bay. And that the shells were roofing it over—bursting toward the fort. If Anderson was obstinate—he was to order the forts on our side to open fire. Certainly fire had begun. The regular roar of the cannon—there it was. And who could tell what each volley accomplished of death and destruction.

The women were wild, there on the housetop. Prayers from the women and imprecations from the men, and then a shell would light up the scene. . . ."

Throughout the North, volunteers rushed to join the Federal army in response to the bombardment of Fort Sumter.

On to Richmond!

NORTH AND SOUTH MOBILIZED AS FOUR MORE STATES SECEDED
AND THE CONFEDERATE CAPITAL WAS ESTABLISHED.

In response to the capture of Fort Sumter, President Lincoln issued a call for 75,000 volunteers to invade the South and "suppress the insurrection." Each state was expected to provide a quota of troops, and men poured forth to defend the Union. North Carolina, Virginia, Tennessee, and Arkansas, the four states of the upper South that were still in the Union, however, balked: They refused to supply troops to invade the Confederacy and would bar Northern armies from crossing into their territory to do so. The four rebel governments promptly seceded and joined the Confederacy, giving the new nation a total of eleven states.

In the South, President Davis called for 150,000 volunteers to defend against Northern invasion. Southerners matched the Union in its patriotic fervor, filling army units with young soldiers ready to defend their homeland.

The conscripts flooded cities and towns in North and South and were sent to huge training camps where they were organized into companies, regiments, brigades, corps, and armies. Although swelling with enthusiasm

and trained on both sides by veterans of the prewar U.S. Army, the volunteers who raced to fight were amateurs.

Predicting Heavy Bloodshed

In May 1861, the Confederate congress voted to move the Confederacy's national capital from backwater Montgomery to Richmond, Virginia, a more populous city that was also a transportation hub, major river port, and a rare Southern industrial center. Relocating the Confederate capital to Virginia guaranteed that the state would become the seat of the conflict, although almost no one in the North or the South expected the war to be long or bloody. Many naive leaders on both sides believed their side would win with a single decisive battle, and within three months. Accordingly, volunteers on both sides were issued 90-day enlistments.

It was commonly boasted in the South that "a lady's thimble will hold all the blood that will be shed"—and one Southern politician famously vowed to drink it. A few thought differently. "This country will be drenched in blood," predicted William T. Sherman, a Northerner

A patriotic lithograph encouraged Northern men to join the army in 1861.

Ready to fight for the Union, an Ohio volunteer armed with a smoothbore musket and fixed bayonet struck a fierce pose for the photographer.

heading a Southern military academy, "and God only knows how it will end." Northern newspaper editorials urged President Lincoln to move quickly, capture the Confederate capital and declare victory. "On to Richmond!" became the battle cry of the Union Forces.

TOP RIGHT: New recruits to the 4th Georgian Infantry assembled beneath the Confederate National Flag in early 1861. Similar scenes occurred throughout the South. BOTTOM RIGHT: Aware that they might never return home, many soldiers had their photo taken, sometimes alone, sometimes with their families.

General Winfield Scott's career mirrored America's military history. He had served in the War of 1812 and the Mexican War and also introduced U.S. troops to Napoleonic strategies.

General Winfield Scott's Derided "Anaconda Plan"

AN AGING MILITARY STRATEGIST ADVISED A NAVAL BLOCKAGE TO BOTTLE UP THE ENTIRE SOUTHERN COASTLINE.

General Winfield Scott, who in 1861 had been general-in-chief of the U.S. Army for twenty years, liked to note that he was one year older than the U.S. Constitution.

His career certainly mirrored the young country's military history. During the War of 1812, Scott was the nation's youngest general, leading the troops against the British. His operations in the Mexican War set a model for a generation of West Pointers. He also authored the military's first tactics manual and its first comprehensive set of regulations. He introduced American troops to Napoleonic battle strategies.

Siding With the Union Cause

A Southerner from Virginia, Scott had chosen to stay with the Union when the nation came apart. During the Fort Sumter crisis, he had advised Lincoln to evacuate the fort as a goodwill gesture to the South and to buy time for Southern emotions to calm. The new president had ignored the advice, however, and appeared more impressed with younger, brasher commanders.

Following the Union's defeat at Fort Sumter, Lincoln turned to Scott for advice and asked for a plan to win the war. What he received in turn ran counter to the popular opinion of the day: The war could indeed be won, but it would be long and potentially bloody.

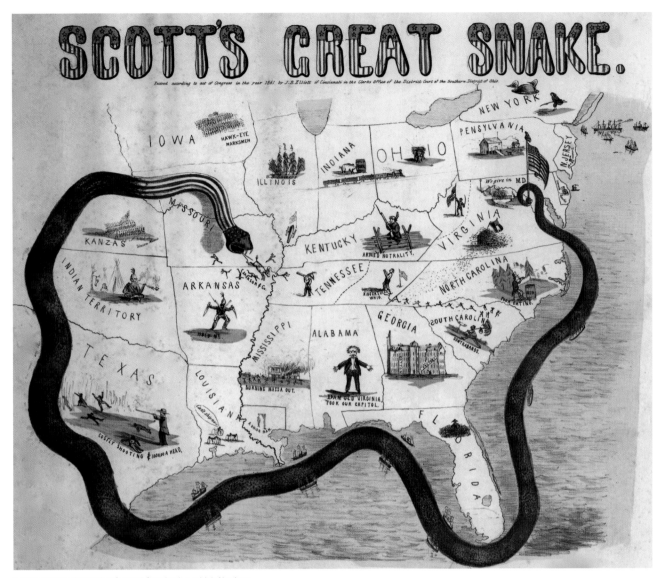

A cartoon map illustrating General Scott's plan, which Northern newspapers laughingly called his "Anaconda Plan." In the end, Scott's maligned strategy would win the war for the North.

Scott's strategy called for a mighty naval blockade that would bottle up the entire Southern coastline on both the Atlantic Ocean and the Gulf of Mexico. The operation would prevent the South from exporting cotton to finance the war and from importing weapons from Britain and France. Meanwhile, a complicated joint army-navy operation would split the Confederacy by capturing the Mississippi River from Memphis to New Orleans. Northern troops would then conquer the South piecemeal until the Confederacy was destroyed. The strategy would take years, Scott explained, but the South would eventually be squeezed to death, as if in the grip of a giant serpent.

Northern newspapers derisively dubbed it the "Anaconda Plan." They also heaped ridicule on the old general and within a few months, General Scott retired. Four years later when the Civil War ended, it was Scott's visionary plan that had led to Northern victory.

EARLY ACTION IN WESTERN VIRGINIA
The war begins with small engagements.

In the summer and fall of 1861, Northern and Southern forces battled for control of the mountainous region of northwestern Virginia, which later became the state of West Virginia. Small but fierce battles were fought at Philippi, Rich Mountain, Carrick's Ford, Carnifex Ferry, and Cheat Mountain.

Beauregard and McDowell Face Off at First Bull Run

INEXPERIENCED SOLDIERS CLASHED IN FEROCIOUS FIGHTING.

In July of 1861, a 37,000-man Northern army lumbered out of its camp near Washington, D.C. and marched through the sweltering summer heat in fits and starts. They were amateurs, led by 42-year-old Brigadier General Irwin McDowell, who had complained to President Lincoln that his men were not ready for battle. "You are green it is true," Lincoln replied, "but [the Confederates] are green also."

The army's destination was Manassas Junction, Virginia, located about 30 miles southwest, where two Southern railroads connected. There McDowell intended to battle 22,000 Confederate troops, commanded by the Southern hero of Fort Sumter, General P.G.T. Beauregard. Trailing McDowell's army out of Washington was a parade of buggies filled with civilians, who cheerfully endured the army's dust so they could see the Southerners thrashed.

Brigadier General Irwin McDowell commanded Federal forces at the Battle of Bull Run. "Victory! Victory!" he shouted at one point—and too soon, events would prove otherwise.

General P.G.T. Beauregard, the Southern hero of Fort Sumter, commanded the Confederate army at Manassas, Virginia—the target of General McDowell's Federal forces.

Brigadier General Joseph E. Johnston and 11,000 Southern troops reached the Bull Run battlefield in time to reinforce Confederate forces.

Bull Run Creek, which cut through the northern Virginia countryside near Manassas Junction, gave the war's first major land battle its name.

BATTLE OF FIRST BULL RUN

Union and Confederate forces collided at Bull Run on July 22, 1861. Blue bars represent Union troop movements; red bars represent Confederates.

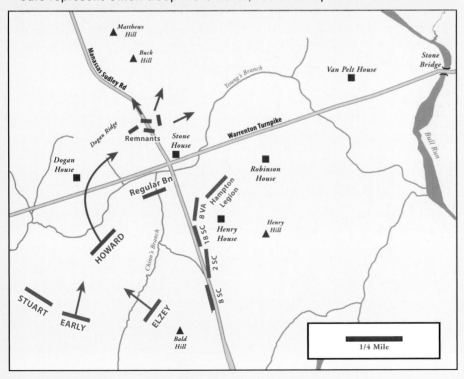

GENERAL IRVIN MCDOWELL
1818–1885

Irvin McDowell had served in the Mexican-American War and been decorated for heroism after the Battle of Buena Vista. Although a career soldier, and a former West Point tactics instructor, McDowell spent much of his career prior to the war in staff roles, and he had no practical experience of higher command in combat situations until his promotion to Brigadier General in 1861. He was relieved of command following the Battle of Second Bull Run.

A Clash of Amateurs

On July 21, 1861, McDowell's army attacked Beauregard's force along Bull Run Creek near Manassas.

At the outset, it appeared the North with its larger force had the upper hand, but at the last minute Beauregard was reinforced by 11,000 troops who were rushed to the scene by rail. After hours of fighting, the Union suddenly slammed into a determined opposition led by Brigadier General Thomas J. Jackson. A 37-year-old former instructor from the Virginia Military Academy, Jackson blasted advancing Union troops with artillery he had amassed atop the battlefield Henry Hill. "Look men!" shouted a Southern officer. "There stands Jackson like a stone wall! Rally behind the Virginians!"

Both sides fought ferociously, but Jackson decided the outcome as Beauregard advanced his entire line. The Federal army folded in retreat, jamming the road back to Washington with wild-eyed soldiers and civilians. Although small in comparison to the bloodbaths that would follow, the 3,600 casualties of the Battle of Bull Run shocked North and South alike. The Civil War's first major land battle had been fought—and it had ended in a spectacular Southern victory.

TOP: Confederate commander Thomas Jonathan Jackson known after the Battle of First Bull Run as "Stonewall."
BOTTOM: At Manassas Junction, a home belonging to Judith Henry Carter was wrecked in battle.

Captured at First Bull Run, Northern prisoners of war posed for a Southern photographer after being shipped to a makeshift prison in Charleston, South Carolina.

After the battle, on the edge of a muddy bog, crude plank headboards were erected over soldiers' graves.

BATTLE OF BALL'S BLUFF

On October 21, 1861, approximately 1,700 Northern troops suffered a humiliating defeat by Southern forces at the Battle of Ball's Bluff, which occurred on the Virginia side of the Potomac River near Washington, D.C. The inexperienced Federal commander, Colonel Edward D. Baker, above—a close friend of President Lincoln—was killed in the battle.

Brigadier General Nathaniel Lyon attempted to rally Northern troops at the Battle of Wilson's Creek, where he was mortally wounded. The dramatic scene was printed in Northern newspapers.

A Bloody Day at Wilson's Creek

THE SOUTH GAINED GROUND IN MISSOURI
UNDER GENERAL BEN MCCULLOCH.

Throughout 1861, Federal and Confederate forces scrambled to control the large border state of Missouri with its important river port of St. Louis. By late summer, Southern forces had been driven into the southwestern corner of the state, near the town of Springfield. There, on August 10, 1861, Northern and Southern armies engaged in the Battle of Wilson's Creek. The battle would later become known as the Bull Run of the West.

Ragtag Soldiers, Experienced Generals
The Northerners were lead by Brigadier General Nathaniel Lyon, a fiery redheaded West Pointer, who launched a surprise attack against a Southern army twice its size. The ambush panicked some of the ragtag Confederates, but not their commander. Brigadier General

Ben McCulloch, a former Texas Ranger and veteran of the prewar U.S. Army, brought up artillery and unleashed a devastating fire that scattered many of Lyon's men as they were looting the Confederate camp.

On another part of the field—on a ridge that would become known as Bloody Hill—General Lyon's attack bogged down into ferocious close-up fighting, and Lyon was trying to hold his own despite two wounds. McCulloch directed a coordinated assault on Lyon's position, and Lyon took a third wound, this one mortal. "Lehmann, I am killed," he stammered to an aide, then fell dead—the first Northern general killed in the war.

Both sides fell back, then the Northern army retreated from the field. The Confederates would not take control of Missouri, but, like First Bull Run in the East, the first major land battle of the West ended in a Confederate victory.

Brigadier General Nathaniel Lyon, commander of Federal forces at the Battle of Wilson's Creek.

Confederate Brigadier General Ben McCullough—victor of the first major land battle in the war's Western Theater.

An illustration depicting the death of General Lyon as he charged the Confederate forces.

GENERALS NATHANIEL LYON

1818–1861

AND BEN MCCULLOCH

1811–1862

Nathaniel Lyon had earned his reputation as a soldier through bloody fighting in California and Kansas.

Ben McCulloch had departed Tennessee for Texas with Davy Crockett, and distinguished himself in the Mexican-American War.

These two career soldiers faced off at the Battle of Wilson's Creek, where Lyon became the first Union general to be killed in action. McCulloch would fall the following year.

3

I HAVE ENTERED THE RANKS

BETWEEN 1861 AND 1865, ALMOST THREE MILLION AMERICAN MEN JOINED FEDERAL OR CONFEDERATE MILITARY SERVICE. ALTHOUGH SOME STRIKING DIFFERENCES EXISTED BETWEEN NORTHERN AND SOUTHERN TROOPS, THEY SHARED AN EXTRAORDINARY AMOUNT IN COMMON.

Members of the 10th Veteran Reserve Corps were deemed unfit for combat due to wounds or illness, but they were still able to play in the corps' band.

"May the Good Lord take care of the poor soldiers."

—A Civil War soldier on the march, 1863

Ready to make the move from civilian life to military service, a crowd of volunteers lined up outside a Northern recruiting station.

Soldiers North and South Rush to Arms

MILITARY LIFE QUICKLY LOST ITS ROMANCE AS TROOPS BATTLED DISEASE, FATIGUE, AND BOREDOM.

Johnny Reb" and "Billy Yank" rushed to war with notions of heroic charges and battlefield bravado. Yet as the newly made soldiers were assembled in training camps throughout the North and South, the reality of military life quickly lost its romance. "We are locked up just like Prisoners," a youthful Yankee wrote home from camp, "and can't get no chance to get out." One of his Rebel counterparts shared his outlook: "This is the damnest place that I ever seen," he wrote.

Many, however, considered military service to be their duty to their country. "Camp life I find to be hard," wrote a Southern recruit, "[but] I will make the best of it." Some gloried in their newfound soldier's life. "I am well and well satisfied," wrote an enthusiastic Rebel. "I weigh one hundred and 40 [and] I am much of a man."

Patriotism, Duty, and a Military Draft

Duty was not the sole motivation for military service in the Civil War. Some Northerners joined the ranks in order to earn government enlistment bonuses. Some Southerners volunteered as paid substitutes for wealthy slave owners.

When the bloodshed drained the manpower, both sides enacted unpopular draft laws. Southerners denounced conscription as a violation of states' rights. The 80 percent who owned no slaves bitterly resented draft exemptions granted to large slave owners.

In the North, the draft was so controversial it sparked riots. In 1863, there was a three-day uprising in New York City that resulted in serious destruction and dozens of deaths.

Many soldiers, however, were genuinely motivated by patriotism or devotion to a cause. For some, ending slavery or defending it was reason enough to enlist. In their letters, Northern soldiers generally cited a heartfelt duty to preserve the Union, while Southerners were mainly motivated to defend home and family and to help achieve Southern nationhood.

KEEPING COUNT

WHO WAS A "TYPICAL" CIVIL WAR SOLDIER?

About 2,000,000 men served in the Northern army, while 750,000 to 1,000,000 fought for the South. Armies on both sides were overwhelmingly white, although the North accepted black soldiers midway through the war and the South tried to do so at war's end.

Three brigades of American Indians fought for the South, and three regiments for the North. The ranks on both sides included many German, Irish, English, and Canadian immigrants, and the Confederacy's Texas regiments included numerous Hispanics.

Most soldiers appear to have been between 18 and 46, although the manpower-short South fielded teenagers and old men.

SOLDIER AGE

Age	Number of Soldiers
Age 13	127
Age 14	330
Age 15	773
Age 16	2,758
Age 17	6,424
Age 18	133,475
Age 19	90,215
Age 20	71,058
Age 21	970,136
Age 45	7,012
Age 46	967
Age 50+	2,366

SOLDIER HEIGHT

Average	5'8 ¼"
Tallest	6'10 ½"
Shortest	3'4"

SOLDIER WEIGHT

Average	143 pounds

ORIGIN OF FOREIGN-BORN SOLDIERS

Nation	Percentage
Germany	35 %
Ireland	30 %
England	10 %
Canada	10 %
Other	15 %

As the war continued, many soldiers North and South came to see war itself as the enemy. They battled, but merely to survive. As Northern victory became increasingly imminent, Southern soldiers shared both their determination and their despair in their letters home, while Northern troops often expressed a renewed sense of purpose. "I can see for myself what this army is for," wrote a young Federal officer, "and what it really does. . . ."

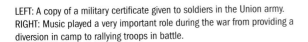

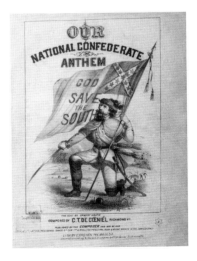

LEFT: A copy of a military certificate given to soldiers in the Union army.
RIGHT: Music played a very important role during the war from providing a diversion in camp to rallying troops in battle.

Most Northern soldiers, like their Southern counterparts were volunteers.

"No Two Keep the Same Step"

JOHNNY REB AND BILLY YANK LEARNED THE WAYS OF WAR.

In camp, soldiers faced daily duties that were often more boring than demanding: There were mind-numbing stints of guard duty, repetitious chores, and seemingly endless hours of drill. But the exercises were vital to train both officers and the rank and file, the vast majority of whom were volunteers with no experience in the military.

For most, their initial performance on the field ranged from comical to deplorable. "Totally undisciplined and undrilled, no two of these men marched abreast," a volunteer officer later recalled. "No two kept the same step; no two wore the same colored coats or trousers."

All Men Are Expected to be in Line

In both the Confederate and Federal armies, the three major branches were infantry, artillery, and cavalry—with most troops serving in the infantry. Some soldiers served in support branches, such as the signal corps, quartermaster department, or engineer corps. All had to adjust to a daily camp routine.

"At daylight in the morning the chief bugler of the regiment sounds the assembly and all the men are expected to be in line to answer to roll call," a Northern cavalryman wrote his sister. "Then another call & we feed & clean horses & get breakfast. At seven comes sick call. At eight comes guard. At noon there is another roll call. At four o'clock, water & feed call again. At sunset dress parade & roll call . . . and at eight o'clock in the evening another flourish of bugles sounds lights out."

Whenever ordered to break camp, infantry troops moved by foot, often on dust-choked roads, in downpours, or through numbing snow and sleet. "It was so dreadful Hot that nobody hardly could Stand it," a Federal drummer wrote home. "I was sunstruck . . . but I got over it." A Southern private wearied from time on the march in debilitating weather simply penned, "May the Good Lord take care of the poor soldiers."

Eventually, the enlisted made the transition from civilian to soldier: By war's end, 750,000 to 1,000,000 Southerners had served in the Confederate armed forces, and more than 2,000,000 Northerners had worn their country's uniform.

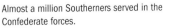

Almost a million Southerners served in the Confederate forces.

Their fixed bayonets glinting in the sun, Federal troops drilled outside their camp on a winter day. Marching and fighting drills were a daily part of life.

Northern soldiers awaited their turn on a camp rifle range. The most common weapon used by both sides was a rifle musket fitted with a bayonet, an improvement over earlier muzzle-loading muskets.

Federal troops in Tennessee lounged outside their winter huts on a sunny day. Temporary camps of makeshift tents were set up most of the year except in winter when soldiers built log huts with small fireplaces to keep warm.

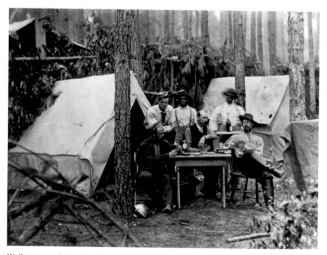

Wall tents and pine bough shelters added a degree of comfort to this early Confederate camp.

Military Discipline Does Not Come Easily

THE RIGOR OF THE SOLDIER'S LIFE WAS A DIFFICULT ADJUSTMENT FOR SOME ENLISTEES.

Military discipline was a new and unusual experience for most Civil War soldiers. Many took to soldiering readily, but others resented authority, and—especially at the beginning of the war—did not hesitate to argue with their officers. Most eventually acquired a passable martial bearing. Some, however, had difficulty submitting to authority—as revealed in a diary entry recorded by Private Edward Burgess of South Carolina:

Quarreled with Capt about breakfast. Said if I got none it would be my fault. Replied it would be his fault, that he never troubled himself to see that the men were properly provided [for]. On inspection said my rifle was dirty. Replied it was clean, having cleaned it three days ago and had not used it since. Gave me an hour to clean it in. replied I would think of it and laughed at him. ordered Lieut to report me. I finally went to him for things to clean it if the State furnished. Said it did not. Would lend me an oiled rag. I did not borrow. However I soaped over the rust and carried it to him. said rifle was in first rate order. I replied that it was no cleaner than before, only soaped over. Went off laughing at him.

Federal army camp cooks worked at a company kitchen in Virginia. Official biweekly rations included 16 ounces of salted beef and 22 ounces of biscuit.

TOP: At a camp in Florida, Southern soldiers whiled away some rare free time.
ABOVE: With mules and supply wagons standing ready, Federal troops underwent training drill.

A Northern army farrier prepared to shoe an officer's mount. In Northern and Southern armies alike, camp chores were endless.

AN ARMY MARCHES ON ITS STOMACH

The official standard biweekly ration for Federal troops consisted of 16 ounces of salted beef or 12 ounces of pork, 22 ounces of biscuit, and 8 quarts of beans, along with coffee, sugar, and vinegar. Official Confederate rations were similar, but were seldom available in the war-stressed South, leaving Confederate troops to feed themselves by foraging. Common Confederate fare was "sloosh"—cornmeal fried in bacon grease.

In close-quartered camps, such as this one occupied by the 1st U.S. Cavalry, contagious illnesses spread quickly, causing staggering loss of life among troops on both sides.

Disease: The War's Most Lethal Enemy

CAMP ILLNESSES TOOK MANY MORE
LIVES THAN BATTLEFIELD DEATHS.

More Civil War soldiers died of illness than bullets. In the confined conditions of the huge camps of the era, contagious diseases spread quickly, especially among the ranks of men from rural areas who had never been exposed to urban illnesses.

The biggest killer was dysentery, which was often caused by inadequate camp hygiene, contaminated drinking water, or poor diet. Other ailments also proved lethal, including measles, pneumonia, typhoid fever, typhus, smallpox, tuberculosis, and a mysterious ailment known only as "the fever," which was later discovered to be mosquito-borne malaria. Most of the war's military operations were in the South, where insect populations were ferocious. "[Of] all the nights I ever spent in the neighborhood of museketoes last night was the worst," wrote a soldier posted to the coast of North Carolina. "No sleep visited my weary eyes until very late."

A Federal burial detail prepared to inter soldiers at a wartime camp near Washington, D.C.

A 17-year-old soldier known only as S. Wires was discharged with typhoid fever, weighing only 90 pounds, after 100 days of service. This photo was taken three weeks after he had returned home.

THERE IS BUT SIX NOW ABLE FOR DUTY

"Hugh has got the measles," wrote a Texas cavalryman from camp. "He has a very bad cold and cough. . . . We carried two from our mess today. There was twelve of us at first. There is but six now able for duty. Four has the measles, one has the chills, one the typhoid newmonia. . . . None of our boys have died yet as I have heard of." Continuous exposure to severe weather and the stress of life in the field also took a toll.

Outside a post chapel in Virginia, fresh graves swelled the size of a soldier cemetery. Of the approximately 620,000 casualties of the Civil War, two-thirds were from disease.

Major Joseph J. Dimock of the 82nd New York Infantry died of disease in June of 1862.

Huge stocks of field artillery, siege mortars, and ordnance were amassed at riverside to arm Federal forces invading Virginia.

New Technology and Old Tactics Reshape the Battlefield

MODERN WEAPONRY MADE KILLING FAR MORE EFFICIENT.

An old soldier would later observe that war was composed of long periods of absolute boredom, interrupted by brief interludes of sheer terror. For many shot dead on the field, their first battle was their last. Survivors, however, could boast that they had "seen the elephant," comparing combat to seeing the highlight of the circus. "The ball was opened," they would say afterward.

Exposure to the horrors of combat could produce a range of emotions: anxiety, fear, excitement, anger, shock, depression, relief, and—for many—even pity for the enemy. "I thought it would do one some good to see dead federals," wrote a Confederate soldier after his first battle. "But I had not seen many until the sight became sickening. I gave my

LEFT: A Southern soldier with a converted flintlock musket. MIDDLE: A Northern cavalryman armed with a rapid-fire, breech-loading Sharps carbine. RIGHT: A heavily armed Northern soldier photographed with a standard-issue 58-caliber Springfield rifle and three Remington revolvers.

canteen of water to a Federal soldier who was badly wounded and felt glad I was able to relieve him."

The Civil War was fought on the opening edge of the Industrial Revolution, and technology had made weaponry much more efficient at killing. Shorter-range smoothbore muskets were being replaced by much more accurate, longer-range rifles, and similar advances also revolutionized artillery.

Yet the common battlefield tactics of the day lagged behind weaponry. In many ways, the Civil War was a 19th-century war fought with 18th-century tactics against 20th-century firearms. Almost 21,000 troops were killed or wounded in a single day at the Battle of Antietam. More than 35,000 were killed or wounded in the three-day Battle of Gettysburg. In eight minutes at the Battle of Cold Harbor, an estimated 7,000 Northern troops were killed or wounded. Such shocking losses made the Civil War—for Americans—the bloodiest war in history. A Confederate general observed, "It wasn't war; it was murder."

Northern rifles stood in a row after the fall of Petersburg in 1865. Soldiers stacked their arms in neat pyramids when not in use to keep them off the ground and easy to retrieve.

Heavy artillery, such as these Confederate smoothbore Columbiads, defended the Southern coastline.

State-of-the art breech-loading Whitworth rifled cannons were imported in small numbers from Britain for the Confederacy.

Marching elbow to elbow in double-rank lines made large numbers of soldiers an easy target for the superior firearms of the day. This resulted in mass casualties as forces faced off.

A Federal surgeon prepared to operate on a wounded soldier following the Battle of Gettysburg.

"There Is No End to These Horrors"

CIVIL WAR MEDICINE OFFERED LITTLE HOPE TO THE WOUNDED. IN SPITE OF THIS
DOCTORS AND NURSES STROVE TO IMPROVE STANDARDS AND SAVE LIVES.

In 1865, 18-year-old Robley Evans, a Northern seaman, was shot through both knees at the Battle of Fort Fisher while making a ground assault with a brigade of naval volunteers. Days later, the ensign found himself in a Federal military hospital facing a drunken surgeon who insisted Evans undergo a double amputation of his legs. After being told that he had no choice, the young sailor reached under his pillow and produced a loaded Colt revolver. "I told him that there were six loads in it," Evans later recalled, "and that if he or anyone else entered my door with anything that looked like a case of instruments I mean to begin shooting."

Evans kept his legs and later recovered. His case was unique: Most soldiers who faced amputations died soon afterward. The state of medical care during the Civil War was enough to make wounded men like Evans resort to desperate measures.

Many doctors and nurses worked heroically to save lives during the war, but they were hampered by the crude state of medical care in the mid-19th century. Effective technologies for treating infectious diseases and trauma injuries did not exist, nor did safeguard practices such as sterilization of instruments. Records show, for example, that one New Hampshire soldier was shot in the shoulder at the Battle of Cedar Creek and received no medical treatment for more than twelve hours. When he finally saw an army surgeon in a field hospital, the doctor jammed a bloody finger in the soldier's entry wound, then poked another bloody finger in the exit wound. When his two fingers touched, the doctor declared his patient fit and sent him on his way.

Of course not all wounded men received such treatment, and in spite of difficult conditions, medical personnel advanced the standards of the day and

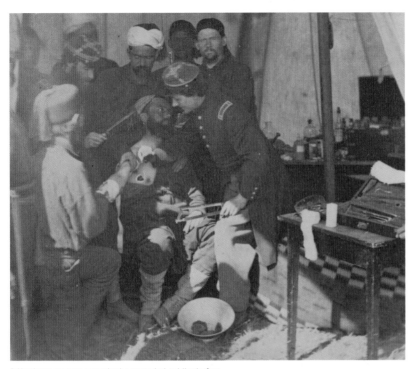

A Northern surgeon consulted a wounded soldier before amputating one of his limbs.

A Southern physician

Tent quarters housed many Federal wounded at City Point, Virginia, where Northern forces established numerous military hospitals.

provided care on an unprecedented scale. The Confederacy constructed the largest hospital at the time, the Chimborazo Hospital in Richmond, which treated 76,000 patients in 150 buildings. The Federal hospital at City Point in Virginia could handle 10,000 patients a day, and boasted a steam laundry.

Still, the enormous casualties frequently left caregivers overwhelmed. "I have been busy all day," wrote a Southern nurse following a major battle, "and I can scarcely tell what I have been doing. I have not taken time even to eat, and certainly not time to sit down. . . . I was going round as usual this morning, washing the faces of the men, and had got half through with one before I found out that he was dead. . . . There is no end to these horrors."

A double amputee. Few soldiers survived amputations.

Nurses tended wounded and ill troops at a Federal field hospital. Around 3,000 women served as nurses for the Union army.

Wounded Northern soldiers crowded a Federal field hospital during the Seven Days Battles in 1862.

WOMEN ON BOTH SIDES STEP IN TO CARE FOR SOLDIERS IN NEED

"I saw for the first time what war meant," wrote Cornelia Hancock, a young Quaker nurse who volunteered to tend wounded soldiers following the Battle of Gettysburg. Hancock was one of approximately 50,000 nurses and attendants who ministered to the wounded and found herself pushing the boundaries of a woman's expected role.

"A woman *must* soar beyond the conventional modesty considered correct under different circumstances," pronounced Phoebe Yates Pember, who became one of the Confederacy's best-known nurses.

Southerner Sally Thompkins so impressed the Confederate congress with her efforts that they commissioned her as an army captain. Leaders in the field for the North were Dorothea Dix, a middle-aged healthcare reformer who was appointed by the U.S. surgeon general to oversee female nurses, and Clara Barton, an independent nurse whose work led to the establishment of the American Red Cross.

On both sides, troops who were seriously wounded or ill were moved from field hospitals to larger, better camp hospitals, such as this.

LEFT: A battlefield station operated by the U.S. Sanitary Commission. RIGHT: Wounded Northern troops werere transported by rail after fighting in the Eastern Theater in 1862.

Medical personnel gathered outside their tent in Camp Letterman, at Gettysburg. Camp Letterman was named after the medical director of the Army of the Potomac, Jonathan Letter, who created the first Ambulance Corps.

Among the Wounded

The U.S. Sanitary Commission, a volunteer organization, promoted improved care for Northern troops, but the work of comforting the sick and wounded fell to female nurses, many who were unprepared for what they would witness.

Alabaman Kate Cumming, who gained renown as a Southern nurse, vividly recorded the shock of her first encounter with a field hospital amputating table: "A stream of blood ran from the table into a tub in which was [an] arm . . . and the hand, which but a short time before grasped the musket . . . was hanging over the edge of the tub—a lifeless thing."

Northern nurse Cornelia Hancock recorded a similar horror in a makeshift federal field hospital at Gettysburg: "Hundreds of desperately wounded men were stretched out on boards laid across the high-backed pews [of a church] as closely as they could be packed together. . . . Thus elevated, these poor sufferers' faces, white and drawn with pain, were almost on a level with my own. I seemed to stand breast-high in a sea of anguish."

CLARA BARTON
1821–1912

A five-foot-tall dynamo from Massachusetts, Clara Barton was working as a clerk in the U.S. Patent Office when the war broke out.

She would soon earn the nickname "Angel of the Battlefield" for her nursing work. She later launched a massive soldier relief effort with donated supplies stored in her Washington, D.C. apartment. The nursing activities she organized to aid countless wounded soldiers and Northern prisoners of war led to the establishment of the American Red Cross.

Private Samuel "Sam" Watkins of Company H, 1st Tennessee Infantry, wrote excellent accounts of battles in his memoir *Company Aytch*.

In this fanciful, romanticized 19th-century artwork, row upon row of soldiers heroically advanced in lockstep motion.

WITNESS TO WAR

The Reality of the Battlefield

ROMANTICIZED VIEWS OF WAR WERE QUICKLY SHATTERED IN THE FACE OF THE HORRORS OF COMBAT.

Mid-19th century Americans commonly held a romanticized image of warfare, popularized by novelists like Sir Walter Scott. They imagined great ranks of uniformed young men emitting excited cheers as they dashed shoulder to shoulder toward the enemy line in an irrepressible charge. Such notions of glory quickly disappeared in the face of the horror and gore of combat. Private Sam Watkins, a Southern soldier, recorded an account of a Confederate assault during the 1864 Battle of Atlanta:

We rushed forward up the steep hillsides, the seething fire from ten thousand muskets and small arms, and forty pieces of cannon hurled right into our very faces . . . piling the ground with our dead and wounded almost in heaps. It seemed that the hot flames of hell were turned loose in all their fury . . . The continued roar of battle sounded like unbottled thunder. Blood covered the ground, and the dense smoke filled our eyes, and ears, and faces. The groans of the wounded and dying rose above the thunder of battle. . . .

I was shot in the ankle and on the heel of my foot. I crawled into [the enemy's] abandoned ditch, which then seemed full and running over with our wounded soldiers. . . .

While I was sitting here, a cannon ball came tearing down the works, cutting a soldier's head off, splattering his brains all over my face and bosom, and mangling and tearing four to five others to shreds. . . .

It was the picture of a real battlefield. Blood had gathered in pools, and in some instances had made streams of blood. 'Twas a picture of carnage and death.

The reality of war: Confederate dead piled following the
1862 Siege of Corinth.

The dismembered body of a Northern solider awaited burial
following the Battle of Gettysburg.

IMMIGRANTS IN THE RANKS

Robust immigration led both
sides to build field military
units that were predominantly
or entirely composed of
Irish or German immigrants.
Major General Franz Sigel,
top, was the highest-ranking
German-American officer in
the Northern army, A German
language recruitment poster,
middle. At the Battle of
Fredericksburg, the North's
famous Irish Brigade, bottom,
engaged Irish-American troops
of the 24th Georgia Infantry.

Led by a Catholic chaplain, Federal troops attended mass in the field.

Confederate Chaplain Robert B. Sutton ministered to soldiers in General Robert E. Lee's Army of Northern Virginia.

Northern Chaplain Thomas Quinn served in the 1st Rhode Island Light Artillery.

Established by the YMCA, the U.S. Christian Commission distributed Bibles, gospel tracts, and songbooks to Northern troops.

Turning to God

EXPRESSIONS OF FAITH BECAME COMMON IN CAMPS AS MILITARY LEADERS ENCOURAGED WORSHIP IN THE NORTH AND THE SOUTH.

As combat wore on, religion came to play an increasing role in soldiers' lives, and Biblical faith was openly expressed in the ranks on both sides. In a single year, the U.S. Christian Commission distributed more than a half-million Bibles to Northern troops.

Commanders routinely mentioned God in official reports, and many publicly shared their faith. General Oliver O. Howard, for instance, often preached on Sundays to his Northern soldiers, and Flag Officer Andrew Foote led worship services for Northern sailors aboard ship.

We Also Have Prayer Meetings Every Night

When Federal forces under his command achieved a victory in 1865, Major General E.R.S. Canby issued an official proclamation urging his troops to set aside the upcoming Sunday as a day of thanksgiving. Prayer meetings, Bible studies, Sunday schools, evening worship services, and baptism services became commonplace. "We have preaching twice every Sunday," a Southern soldier wrote home. "We also have prayer meeting every night."

General Stonewall Jackson personally handed out gospel tracts in camp. General Robert E. Lee issued orders excusing Jewish troops from Saturday duty so they could participate in Sabbath worship, and officially called for periods of prayer and fasting in his army. Said Lee: "I am nothing but a poor sinner, trusting in Christ alone for salvation."

An Impromptu Blue and Gray Choir

Huge revivals swept through the Southern armies in 1862 through 1864, sometimes drawing open-air crowds numbering in the thousands.

Although the wartime revivals were largely a Southern phenomenon, Northern and Southern soldiers were generally linked by a common faith. For instance, when Confederate soldiers gathered on a Virginia riverbank for a baptism at one point, Northern troops appeared on the opposite side to watch—then spontaneously joined the Southerners in a familiar hymn. When the impromptu blue and gray choir finished singing, troops on both riverbanks quietly returned to duty.

The 54th Massachusetts Infantry was the first Northern regiment of black troops. The 54th earned enduring fame for its costly assault on Battery Wagner in 1863.

"They Met Death Coolly, Bravely"

BLACK TROOPS TOOK UP ARMS FOR THE NORTH.

Black Americans were among the first to volunteer for military service in the Civil War but neither government welcomed them initially.

In New Orleans in 1861, more than 1,100 African-American freedmen responded to the Louisiana governor's call for volunteers, and formed the 1st Louisiana Native Guard to fight for the Confederacy. But the state declined to provide arms and equipment, and when the freedman provided their own, the state legislature passed a law prohibiting black regiments. The

Native Guard was disbanded, then re-formed after Federal troops captured and occupied New Orleans in 1862—this time to fight for the Union. Confederate officials remained still uninterested in fielding black troops.

The Union was only slightly more enthusiastic. President Lincoln was initially reluctant to allow African-Americans to serve in the Federal armies, fearing it would offend border state slaveholders who were loyal to the Union. Eventually, he changed his mind, and in 1863, the U.S. Army aggressively began recruiting

A slave identified only as "Marlboro" accompanied Major Raleigh S. Camp to war with the 40th Georgia Infantry and was photographed in a Confederate uniform.

Untold numbers of "body servants" and other slaves accompanied affluent Southerners to war. Silas Chandler, right, a family slave, was photographed with Sergeant A.M. Chandler of the 44th Mississippi Infantry.

An unidentified young black recruit in the 103rd Regiment of the U.S. Colored Troops stood proudly for a photograph.

black Americans into a segregated force that was officially known as the U.S. Colored Troops. They were organized into 166 black regiments, including thirteen artillery regiments, seven cavalry regiments, a regiment of engineers, and 145 infantry regiments.

Brave Company

By regulation, Northern black troops were led by white officers, and for much of the war they received less than half the pay issued to white soldiers. Many Union commanders questioned blacks' ability to participate in combat, and used them mainly to clear brush or as backup reserves.

When they were placed in battle, however, African-American troops quickly proved themselves. "I never saw a braver company of men in my life," reported Captain M.M. Miller, who commanded U.S. Colored Troops at the Battle of Milliken's Bend in 1863. "They met death coolly, bravely," he stated. "All were steady and obedient to orders. . . ." Black troops in the Federal army and black landsmen in the U.S. Navy made significant contributions to the eventual Northern victory, and more than twenty African-American soldiers were awarded the U.S. Congressional Medal of Honor.

Confederates Finally Open the Ranks

Not until 1863, when the war was bleeding away Southern manpower, did the Confederacy begin to consider recruiting black troops into the ranks. A group of Confederate officers informally made the suggestion, but it was ignored. The idea was officially proposed, then shot down by the congress in 1864. Finally, in March of 1865, under pressure from General Robert E. Lee, Confederate lawmakers authorized the organization of 300,000 freed slaves into Southern military service.

"It is however of primary importance," Lee advised, "that . . . they should be so treated as to feel that their obligations are those of any other soldier. . . . Harshness and contemptuous or offensive language or conduct toward them must be forbidden. . . ." In Richmond, African-American recruits began drilling for service. However, the South's effort came too late. The war ended before black Confederate regiments could be fielded in combat.

Their names lost to history, a soldier posed with his wife and daughters for a wartime family photograph.

LEFT: A young black sailor in the U.S. Navy. RIGHT: By 1865, more than 90,000 black Americans were serving in the Northern army.

Black soldiers of the 1st U.S. Colored Troops assembled for drill. The North's black regiments were all commanded by white officers.

Sergeant Thomas Strawn served in the 3rd Heavy Artillery, a regiment of the U.S. Colored Troops that was recruited in Union-occupied Tennessee.

A black Northern non-commissioned officer

Soldiers of the 107th U.S. Colored Troops were recruited in Federal-occupied Kentucky, and served in North Carolina and Virginia.

"Jackson," a drummer in the 79th U.S. Colored Troops

Northern black troops "met death coolly," it was said.

At war's end, the 4th U.S. Colored Troops manned the defenses protecting Washington, D.C.

Northern guards assembled for a photograph at Indiana's Camp Morton, where more than 1,700 Southern prisoners of war died of illness and exposure.

Capture Is As Deadly As Combat

PRISONERS OF WAR FACED STARVATION, EXPOSURE, AND DISEASE.

For soldiers in the Civil War, becoming a prisoner of war could almost be as risky as entering combat. An estimated 56,000 troops died in captivity during the course of the war, about 26,000 Southerners and 30,000 Northerners. Illness—especially dysentary—killed the most prisoners, while many died from exposure and others starved.

In the South, Confederate troops were often short on rations, and their prisoners of war fared even worse. "I recollect some half a dozen naked forms, out of which the likeness of human beings had been starved away," recalled a Union survivor of South Carolina's Florence Stockade. "[They were] groping around in prison without a shirt to their backs, with chattering teeth, their gaze idiotic, and their speech confused and incoherent."

News of the deadly conditions in Southern prison camps led the Lincoln administration to retaliate by reducing rations for Southern prisoners of war, causing increased suffering and death. "The poor fellows died rapidly, despondent, homesick, hungry and wretched," recounted one Southerner at New York's Elmira Prison. "I have stood day after day watching the wagons carrying the dead outside to be buried. . ."

Conditions worsened on both sides in 1863, when Northern authorities halted prisoner exchanges in an attempt to cripple Southern manpower and to protest the Confederacy's refusal to recognize captured black troops as POWs. When the exchanges stopped, the Confederacy was overwhelmed by the logistical challenge of feeding a larger prison population. At the Salisbury Prison in North Carolina, where prisoner deaths had once been rare, more than 3,000 Northern POWs perished over the course of a year. Other prisons also recorded grievous death rates.

TOP: Georgia's Camp Sumter, infamously known as Andersonville Prison, was the deadliest of all Civil War POW camps. ABOVE: More than 12,000 Northern soldiers died in the crowded confines of Andersonville.

The day's dead were buried in a trench at Andersonville. Approximately 26,000 Southern prisoners perished during the war, and 30,000 Northerners died in prison.

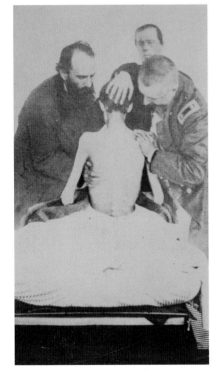

ABOVE: Prisoners at Camp Douglas. Southern POW camps could not properly care for their swelling populations.

LEFT: Newly released from captivity in the South, a Northern soldier was examined by U.S. Army doctors.

WHO WERE SUTLERS?
War profiteeers or merchants of comfort?

Sutlers, merchants authorized to trade with soldiers, were a fixture on Northern army posts, naval stations, and in camp and field. They were both loved and hated by the troops. While the men were glad to obtain tobacco, toothbrushes, postage stamps, newspapers, molasses, dried fruit, canned meat, pies, and cakes, they despised the inflated prices the sutlers charged.

TOP: Northern photographer Samuel A. Cooley and his assistants posed beside their camera and equipment wagon. Cooley accompanied Northern forces into the U.S. Army's Department of the South, which included South Carolina, Georgia, and Florida. BOTTOM: The Civil War's most famous photographer, Mathew Brady, leaned against a pine tree, far right, and observed Northern officers in a field conference.

A respected and award-winning photographer before the war, Mathew Brady set out to document the conflict in pictures. His photographs of the carnage would shock the nation.

At his own expense, Brady set up teams of staff to follow troops into battle, acting as the first field photographers.

Civil War Photography

PHOTOGRAPHIC TECHNOLOGY CHANGED
THE WAY WE SEE AND UNDERSTAND WAR.

"I had the chance to go to town yesterday evening to have my picture taken," a Southern soldier wrote his wife in 1861. "I am going to send it to you."

Photography was a new and popular technology in the mid-19th century, and the Civil War became the first conflict in history to be thoroughly recorded by the camera. Photographic field equipment was expensive and bulky and had to be transported by wagon. When a photograph was made, any movment would cause an image to blur, so capturing battlefield action was almost impossible. Even so, an enterprising handful of photographers took their cameras to the field and masterfully recorded pictures of armies, fortifications, troops, artillery, and other stationary subjects.

Thousands of images were taken. Some photographers published theirs on inexpensive cardboard and sold them as *"cartes de visite,"* which became immensely popular with the public. Others held public exhibitions of their photographs that included images of battlefield dead, leaving viewers both fascinated and shocked.

Brady & Co.

The most famous Civil War photographer was Mathew Brady, who had studios in New York City and Washington, D.C. Brady's reputation and his location in Washington gave him easy access to many of the war's leaders and to the battlefields in Virginia. Other leading Northern photographers were Alexander Gardner, Timothy O'Sullivan, and George N. Barnard, all of whom had worked for Brady at some point.

Southern Photographers Capture the War

In the South, photographic equipment and chemicals were hard to come by, but some Southern photographers still managed to record the war. George S. Cook of South Carolina, also a former Brady man, settled in Charleston on the eve of the war. Cook captured early images of Fort Sumter, and later drew fire from Federal warships while taking photographs of coastal fortifications. New Orleans photographer

ABOVE LEFT: Photographer George N. Barnard, who was embedded with Northern forces in the field, recorded daily life in the army, such as these soldiers protecting their encampment. ABOVE RIGHT: Barnard eventually embedded with General William T. Sherman and his troops. Among their stops was Fort Sumter, South Carolina, pictured here after its capture by Union forces.

MIDDLE: Capturing action on the battlefield was virtually impossible with early equipment, so photographers turned to still subjects. The horse and rider here had to freeze for several seconds while the shot was taken. BOTTOM: Photographer George Barnard was with General William T. Sherman's army when it captured Atlanta. He published these photos in *Photographic Views of Sherman's Campaign*.

J.D. Edwards also took his camera into the field, and recorded early images of Southern troops, camps, and fortifications at Pensacola, Florida.

Portrait Photographers Also Visually Recorded the War, One Person at a Time

Meanwhile, portrait photographers created an equally important record of the Civil War by capturing countless individual soldiers and civilians across the country.

Loved ones at home wanted keepsake photographs of the menfolk going off to war, new recruits were eager to be photographed in uniform, and soldiers wanted images of sweethearts, wives, and children to carry with them into battle. Photographs were produced in a variety of formats—including the inexpensive cartes de visite, costlier tintypes, and pricey daguerreotypes or ambrotypes. Quite small in size, daguerreotypes captured an image directly onto a polished silver-coated copper plate, giving it a mirrored appearance. To prevent tarnish, daguerreotypes were always stored in protective cases. Cheaper to produce were ambrotypes, which were printed onto emulsion-coated glass and required a painted or fabric background to frame the image. The small size of these early photographs made them ideal, portable keepsakes for soldiers.

LEFT: Photographer Timothy O'Sullivan was an apprentice at Mathew Brady's gallery in New York. He then joined Brady's team of photographers when the Civil War started. Later in the war he teamed up with Alexander Gardner's studio, which published his work. RIGHT: In 1865, O'Sullivan traveled to North Carolina to document the siege of Fort Fisher, shown here after being crushed by Union forces.

George S. Cook, an adventuresome South Carolina photographer, captured numerous rare photographs of Southerners at war, including this image of Confederate artillerymen at their post near Charleston.

LOUIS DAGUERRE

1787–1851

Louis-Jacques-Mandé Daguerre was a French designer, painter, and inventor. He became known in the 1820s when he helped develop the Diorama Theater, but today is best remembered for creating a more efficient method of developing photographs known as daguerrotypes.

At the time, the process could take multiple hours, but using Daguerre's solution of silver, mercury, and salt, a photographer could develop a daguerreotype in only twenty or thirty minutes. His name is inscribed on the Eiffel Tower.

Inexpensive cartes de visite—albumin prints on paper backed by cardboard—such as those above, were popular with civilians and soldiers in both North and South. Lightweight and the size of a business card, they were easy to send by mail, and people often collected them like calling cards.

Due to the naval blockade, photographs were significantly more expensive in the South. As a result, there are fewer portraits of Confederate soldiers and their families than there are Union ones.

A Rare Comfort in War Time

Having one's image captured by a photographer was seen as an important, serious event. The subject had to hold an unflinching pose to avoid blurring the image, and the powder flash that provided lighting could be startling—few smiles appeared in Civil War photographs.

For soldiers and civilians alike, however, having a picture of an absent loved one was worth the trouble and expense. "I look at your likeness and fear it is the last time I shall see you," a wife wrote her soldier husband in 1862. Their toddler, she reported, "will look at it and kiss it all the time." In camp and on the battlefield, the image of a familiar, beloved could bring rare comfort. For some soldiers, looking at a photograph was a final act. "Splinters flew from fences and rocks," recalled a survivor of an enemy artillery barrage. "One young soldier was killed with the portrait of his sister in his hand."

Photography and printing techniques evolved during the late 1800s to become easier, faster, and cheaper. Tintypes, top left; ambrotypes, top right and bottom left; daguerrotypes, middle; and photographis printed on paper, bottom right, were in high demand.

4 1862: A COUNTRY TORN ASUNDER

DURING THE SECOND YEAR OF THE CIVIL WAR THE NORTH STEADILY ADVANCED IN THE WESTERN THEATER, WHILE THE SOUTH TRIUMPHED IN THE EAST. THE CONFLICT'S UNPRECEDENTED CARNAGE SHOCKED AMERICANS EVERYWHERE.

Some 23,000 were killed or injured during the Battle of Antietam. Here Confederate dead awaited burial in front of Dunker Church.

"It is well that war is so terrible—we should grow too fond of it."

—Confederate general Robert E. Lee, December 13, 1862

LEFT: Ulysses S. Grant married Julia Dent in 1848. The two met through Dent's brother Frederick, a friend of Grant's from West Point. Dent, the daughter of a plantation owner from St. Louis, often traveled to visit Grant during wartime. RIGHT: The couple had four children. Frederick was their oldest, followed by Ulysses Jr., Nellie, and Jesse.

Grant Rises to Command

AFTER A SLOW START TO HIS MILITARY CAREER, GRANT
SUCCEEDED AS A LEADER OF THE U.S. ARMY.

On the eve of the Civil War, Ulysses S. Grant was peddling firewood on a street corner in St. Louis. Anyone passing his woodpile who gave him a second glance scarcely would have imagined that the rumpled, bearded salesman would be commanding general of all U.S. armies in less than five years, and that within another five would be president of the United States.

Born in 1822 in southern Ohio, where his father operated a tannery, Hiram Ulysses Grant grew up amid the hardy roughness of the rural Midwest. Grant's father used his connections with Ohio congressman Elihu B. Washburne to wrangle his son an appointment to West Point. Young Grant was a mediocre student—

excelling only in horsemanship—but he still graduated in the class of 1843.

As a second lieutenant, Grant was posted to Jefferson Barracks outside of St. Louis, where he met and eventually married Julia Dent, the sister of his former West Point roommate and a cousin to future Confederate general James Longstreet. The Grants would have four children—and they would also come to own several slaves, most of whom were given to Julia by her father. Grant was an unenthusiastic slaveholder, and freed the one slave in his name before the war.

He distinguished himself in the Mexican-American War as a junior officer, and was commended for his

In 1843, Ulysses S. Grant graduated from West Point as a second lieutenant in the U.S. Army. He was ranked 21 in a class of 39.

courage. Afterward, Grant was assigned to various army posts, and was eventually transferred to Fort Humboldt in California. There, separated from his family, he fell into heavy drinking, and—with official censure possibly looming—he resigned from the army in 1854.

Never Fearing the Enemy

In civilian life, Grant struggled to support his family and drifted from one job to another. At times, he was assisted by his father and father-in-law. He took up farming, the staple of 19th-century occupations, but failed at that too. He made ends meet by selling firewood, and pawned his gold pocket watch for cash. He was working at his father's leather goods store in

1862

The War Widens

January 1862 brought with it a new level of bloodshed.

February 6 Fort Henry fell to Federal army-navy forces.

February 16 Fort Donelson surrendered to General Ulysses S. Grant.

March 9 CSS *Virginia* and USS *Monitor* engaged in first battle of ironclad ships.

March 17 General George B. McClellan began the Union's Peninsula Campaign.

April 6–7 The Confederates launched a surprise attack against General Ulysses S. Grant's army at the Battle of Shiloh.

April 7 Island No. 10 surrendered to Federal forces, opening the Mississippi River to the Union navy as far as Fort Pillow.

May

April 25 U.S. Navy captured New Orleans cutting off the South from one of its major ports.

June 25–July 1 In the campaign known as the Seven Days' Battles, Robert E. Lee forced the Union army to retreat away from Richmond.

August 28–30 The Confederates secured another victory at the Second Battle of Bull Run.

September 17 The Battle of Antietam was the first major battle to occur on Union soil.

September

September 22 President Lincoln announced Emancipation Proclamation freeing the slaves in the Southern states.

December 13 The Union army sustained massive casualties in a defeat at the Battle of Fredericksburg.

December

Major General Ulysses S. Grant with his favorite mount, Cincinnati.

EDWIN M. STANTON
1814–1869

In 1862, President Lincoln appointed Edwin M. Stanton as secretary of war. The burly Stanton aggressively pushed the Northern war effort, firing generals for Lincoln and pushing him to field black troops. Although controversial and overbearing, Stanton was a key contributor to the eventual Union victory.

the upper Mississippi River port of Galena, Illinois, when the Civil War began. The war rescued Ulysses Grant. Experienced officers were in demand, especially West Pointers, and after commanding a regiment of Ohio troops as a colonel, Grant managed to obtain a brigadier general's commission with the assistance of Congressman Washburne.

The years of failure had shaped Grant's character: He was now determined to succeed. As a troop commander in the opening days of the war, he convinced himself never to fear the enemy. "I never forgot," he later said, "that he had as much reason to fear my forces as I had his."

Grant handled himself capably with early commands, then gained attention with a successful attack on a Confederate camp in eastern Missouri. That engagement, which became known as the Battle of Belmont, positioned Grant as a bold commander who was willing to take risks to win. In the spring of 1862, General Ulysses S. Grant found himself commanding tens of thousands of Northern troops—with orders to strike deeper into the Southern heartland.

In 1864, Major General Ulysses S. Grant, the former firewood peddler,
was appointed commanding general of all Northern armies.

Federal gunboats provided artillery support for army operations against Forts Henry and Donelson.

Grant Attacks Forts Henry and Donelson

UNION FORCES TOOK THE OFFENSIVE IN TENNESSEE, AIMING TO SEIZE THE MISSISSIPPI RIVER AND SPLIT THE CONFEDERACY.

By early 1862, the war was divided into three principal regions or "theaters" of operations: the Eastern Theater roughly covered the Atlantic coast to the Appalachians; the Western Theater stretched from the Appalachians to the Mississippi River; and the Trans-Mississippi Theater covered everything from the Mississippi westward.

In the Western Theater, the Union high command determined that the best way to conquer the Southern heartland was to utilize its rivers. They planned for Northern forces to advance along the Cumberland and Tennessee Rivers, capture Tennessee and the upper South, then seize the Mississippi River and split the Confederacy.

The first targets were a pair of Confederate defensive strongholds. Forts Henry and Donelson lay 12 miles apart in northwest Tennessee. Fort Henry overlooked the Tennessee River, and the more formidable Fort Donelson commanded a high bluff over the Cumberland River. To capture them, a joint Federal army-navy operation was launched under the command of a scruffy, obscure Northern officer with a checkered past—Brigadier General Ulysses S. Grant.

Inundated by unusually high winter floodwaters and pounded by navy gunboats, Fort Henry quickly surrendered. Grant then attacked Fort Donelson. The ranking Confederate commanders fled their post, leaving Brigadier General Simon Buckner—an old army friend of Grant's—to surrender the fort. When Buckner asked for terms, Grant famously wrote back: "No terms except an unconditional and immediate surrender can be accepted. I propose to move immediately on your front." Buckner surrendered the fort to Grant's forces.

I Can't Spare This Man—He Fights.

The Federal victories at Forts Henry and Donelson broke the Confederate defensive line, ensuring that the neutral border state of Kentucky would be held by Northern forces. This led to the capture of Nashville, the capital of Tennessee, and successfully opened the Southern heartland to invasion. The first major Northern victory of the war, it earned Grant a promotion to major general and made him a national hero in the North. In Washington, Lincoln said of Grant: "I can't spare this man—he fights."

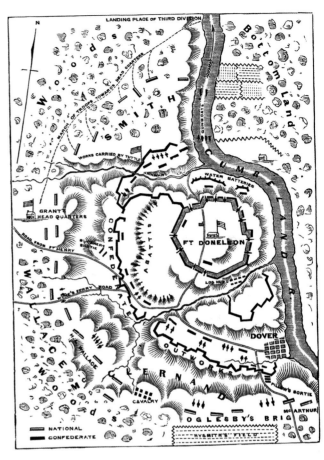

ABOVE: Then–Brigadier General Ulysses S. Grant posed for a portrait early on in the war. His victories at Forts Henry and Donelson opened the South to invasion.
RIGHT: Located on a high ridge above the Cumberland River, Fort Donelson was a well-built and well-guarded Southern fortress.

Flag Officer Andrew H. Foote, U.S.N. bombarded Fort Henry into submission.

Confederate Brigadier General Simon B. Buckner was an old army friend of Union general Ulysses S. Grant.

An illustration depicting Federal forces attempting to turn back a Confederate assault at the Battle of Shiloh.

A Bloody Disaster for the South

ON APRIL 6, 1862 CONFEDERATE FORCES STRUCK
THE UNION ARMY OF THE TENNESSEE.

Flush with victory after capturing Forts Henry and Donelson, Grant moved his newly named Army of the Tennessee southward on the Tennessee River, supported by U.S. Navy gunboats. Their first stop was Savannah in southwest Tennessee, where they were joined by other Northern forces. They planned to attack nearby Corinth, Mississippi, a center on a vital rail line that extended across the upper South.

But on April 6, 1862, before Grant could act, he was caught off guard by 44,000 Confederate troops under General Albert Sidney Johnston. Many Union troops abandoned their camps in panic and ran for the rear. Fighting was fierce, and slowly the Confederates pushed Grant's men back towards the Tennessee River. The combat was especially vicious around the white-washed Shiloh Church, which would give the battle its name, and

it appeared that Grant was on the verge of defeat.

But in the midst of battle, Johnston—who was directing his troops on horseback—suddenly slumped in his saddle, and died. His frantic aides could find no wound on his body, until they pulled off the general's thigh-high cavalry boots and discovered that he had taken a bullet in the leg. By choosing to ignore the injury, Johnston had bled to death in his boot.

His second-in-command, General P.G.T. Beauregard—of Fort Sumter and Bull Run fame—took charge, but it was not enough to turn the tide.

During the night, 25,000 fresh troops arrived to bolster the Union position and the next day, April 7, Grant launched a strong counterattack. When Southern reinforcements failed to arrive, General Beauregard reluctantly retreated.

Federal artillery batteries such as this one played a critical role
in resisting the Confederate attack at Shiloh.

Attired in blue uniforms, Confederate officers from the Washington Artillery of New Orleans stood at
attention outside their tent. The unit suffered serious casualties at Shiloh.

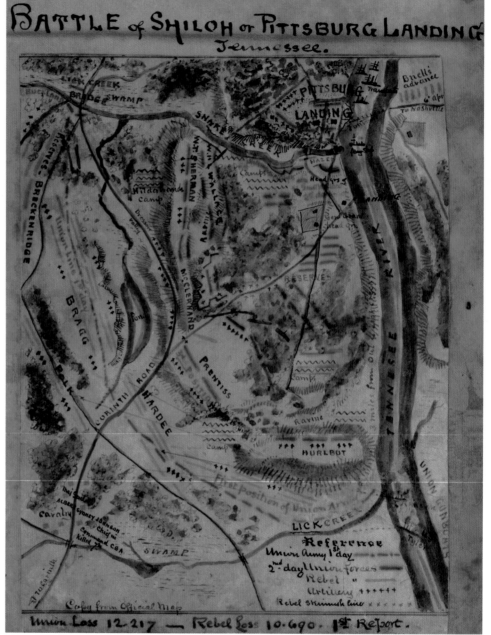

A map of the Battle of Shiloh, the southern name for the Battle of Pittsburg landing.

THE WILD WEST

Northern and Southern forces waged war even in the faraway West, in fights like The Battle of Glorieta Pass in the Northern New Mexico. On March 28, 1862, Confederate troops attacked Union soldiers, with the hope of capturing Fort Union and breaking the Union army's stronghold in the Southwest. But the Northerners, under the overall command of Brigadier General E.R.S. Canby, prevailed and prevented the Confederates from invading California.

Signs Of A Long And Bloody War

More than 100,000 troops were engaged at Shiloh, making it the largest battle ever waged in America at the time. Its 23,000 casualties stunned both sides, and everyone realized that they faced a long and bloody war. Although both armies claimed to have won at Shiloh, the battle proved to be a major strategic victory for the North: It forced the Confederates to abandon much of Tennessee, enabled Federal forces to later capture the important Southern rail center at Corinth, opened the way to conquering the Mississippi River, and cost the Confederacy the leadership of Albert Sidney Johnston.

General P.G.T. Beauregard took charge of the Southern attack at Shiloh after Johnston was killed in action.

General Albert Sidney Johnston was considered the greatest soldier then living.

Pittsburg Landing—shown here with the USS *Tycoon*, right, and *Tigress*, second from the right, docked in 1862—was the landing site for ships carrying supplies and reinforcements for the Union army.

GENERAL ALBERT SIDNEY JOHNSTON

1803–1862

A tall, impressive-looking Kentuckian, Johnston was the senior Confederate commander in the Western Theater. A veteran of the Mexican-American War, he had been seasoned in high-ranking posts in the prewar U.S. Army, and was viewed as America's foremost military commander on the eve of the war. He was offered second-in-command of all Northern forces, but instead chose to side with the South. President Jefferson Davis would later call him "the greatest soldier, the ablest man, civil or military, Confederate or Federal, then living."

A Bloodless Victory for the North

ISLAND NO. 10 FELL AND GAVE UNION FORCES
A STRONGHOLD IN THE MISSISSIPPI RIVER.

"The Mississippi is the backbone of the
Confederacy," President Lincoln observed early
in the war. "It is the key to the whole situation."

Despite his lack of military experience, Lincoln quickly
proved himself to be a natural military strategist and
a superb commander in chief. He soon realized the
importance of one element of General Winfield Scott's
lampooned Anaconda Plan: Capturing the Mississippi
River would split the South and irreparably damage the
Confederacy. Accordingly, Lincoln pressed his military

commanders to prioritize conquering the waterway.

The initiative unfolded under the direction of General
John Pope, who besieged Island No. 10, a powerful
Confederate fortification built on an island in the
Mississippi where the river coursed along Tennessee's
northwest corner.

Named for its position as the tenth island south of
Cairo, Illinois, the island was key to the Confederacy's
Mississippi River defenses. In an innovative maneuver,
General Pope surrounded and isolated the Confederates

Federal gunboats bombarded Confederate
defenses at Island No. 10.

Brigadier General John Pope's innovative attack on Island No. 10 secured the
Mississippi stronghold for Union forces.

ISLAND NUMBER TEN

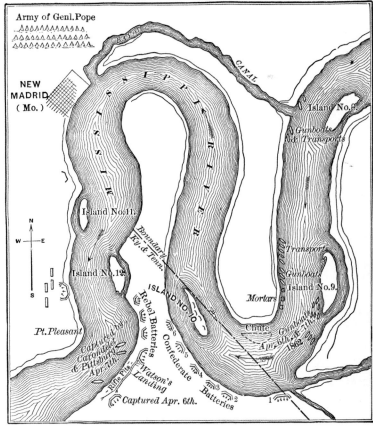

MAP OF ISLAND NUMBER TEN.

from the rear, with the help of naval
gunboats. The Southerners gave up
without a fight on April 7, 1862—the same
day that Confederate forces were forced to
withdraw at the Battle of Shiloh.

For the North, it was an important and
largely bloodless victory: While the South
surrendered more than 4,500 troops and
a huge amount of heavy artillery, Federal
casualties amounted to less than 30.

Rear Admiral David G. Farragut, right, stood at the wheel of his flagship, the USS *Hartford*.

New Orleans Falls

NORTHERN FORCES CAME EVER CLOSER TO SEIZING
THE MISSISSIPPI RIVER FROM THE CONFEDERATES.

On April 25, 1862—less than three weeks after the Northern triumphs at Shiloh and Island No. 10—the vitally important Southern port city of New Orleans fell to a Northern joint army-navy expedition.

The victory, engineered by Captain David G. Farragut, illustrated the importance the North's naval superiority played throughout the war. The attack began on April 18, when Farragut dispatched 17 warships and 21 mortar boats to batter New Orleans' coastal defenses. Backed by a 13,000-man army under Major General Benjamin F. Butler, Farragut unleashed a barrage of artillery projectiles aimed at the city's two heavily-armed fortifications, Fort Jackson and Fort Saint Philip, which lay below the city on opposite sides of the Mississippi River. "The work of destruction was incessant," noted Fort Jackson's commander Brigadier General Johnson K. Duncan.

Captain Farragut forced the surrender of the famous Crescent City. The Confederate commander at New Orleans, Major General Mansfield Lovell, ordered all military depots destroyed, and retreated. The South had lost its largest city and main Gulf Coast seaport.

Soon afterward, the river port of Memphis on the upper Mississippi suffered a similar fate, leaving only the Southern stronghold of Vicksburg, Mississippi as the principal Confederate defender of the Mississippi River. Northern forces were closing in.

David G. Farragut commanded the naval attack against New Orleans. He was rewarded for his success with the title of rear admiral and was the first person to hold the rank in the U.S. Navy.

Major General Benjamin F. Butler took control of the city once it was in Union hands. He acted as military governor there until December 1862, when he was removed due to controversial decisions.

MIDDLE: Steamboats lined the levee at New Orleans in 1862. BOTTOM: Admiral Farragut's Federal fleet attacked the Confederate defenses at New Orleans in this Civil War–era artwork.

Commander of the Confederate forces at New Orleans, Major General Mansfield Lovell was an unpopular choice among the locals when appointed to his position. Lovell was blamed for losing the city, and the battle ended his military career.

Northern sailors re-coaled naval vessels on the lower Mississippi.

A Beast of a General

THE CONTROVERSIAL MILITARY LEADER BENJAMIN BUTLER TOOK CONTROL OF
NEW ORLEANS ISSUING COMMANDS THAT PROVOKED SOUTHERN OUTRAGE.

When New Orleans surrendered to Federal forces in 1862, it was placed under the command of perhaps the most controversial officer in the U.S. Army, Major General Benjamin F. Butler.

A middle-aged, former Massachusetts lawyer, Butler had been granted the rank of general thanks to his political connections. He was fat and balding and famously eccentric, given to wearing bedroom slippers and reciting poetry aloud while riding around at night. A critic once described him as "as helpless as a child on the field of battle and as visionary as an opium-eater."

Butler was often erratic. In New Orleans, he ordered a man hanged for allegedly desecrating the American flag, illegally seized 1 million dollars from the French consulate, and was accused of amassing a fortune in stolen Southern silverware—a charge that earned him the nickname Spoons Butler.

His most infamous controversy, however, was the "Woman's Order." During the time Butler commanded New Orleans, his officers repeatedly complained of being insulted by the city's female residents. The women reportedly forced the men off the sidewalks and insulted them with snide remarks. The last straw came when a woman leaned out an upstairs window and emptied a chamber pot on the head of Captain David Farragut, the commander of U.S. naval operations in New Orleans. In retaliation, Butler ordered any woman who insulted a Northern soldier to be arrested as a prostitute.

News of the command enraged the South: "Beast Butler" was angrily denounced in Southern newspapers, and President Davis ordered him to be shot on sight as an outlaw. Federal authorities eventually found another command post for the general. Southern crockery makers, meanwhile, boosted sales by adorning the inside of their chamber pots with images of Butler.

B-19

Major General Benjamin F. Butler, the Federal commander of occupied New Orleans, scandalized the South when he ordered any New Orleans women who insulted Northern officers to be arrested as prostitutes.

BUTLER'S PROCLAMATION

An outrageous insult to the Women of New Orleans!

Southern Men, avenge their wrongs!!!

Head-Quarters, Department of the Gulf, New Orleans, May 15, 1862.

General Orders, No. 28.

As the Officers and Soldiers of the United States have been subject to repeated insults from the women calling themselves ladies of New Orleans, in return for the most scrupulous non-interference and courtesy on our part, it is ordered that hereafter when any Female shall, by word, gesture, or movement, insult or show contempt for any officer or soldier of the United States, she shall be regarded and held liable to be treated as a woman of the town plying her avocation.

By command of Maj.-Gen. BUTLER,
    GEORGE C. STRONG,
        A. A. G. Chief of Staff.

The "Stars and Stripes" flew over captive New Orleans.

Over the course of the war, more than 400 locomotives operated under the U.S. Military Railroads.

Victory Rides the Rails

EFFECTIVE USE OF RAILWAYS BOOSTED
NORTHERN MILITARY OPERATIONS.

The North's railway system, which was far superior to its Southern counterpart in scope and technology, made a major contribution to the Northern campaign. For example, when Northern forces were defeated at the 1863 Battle of Chickamauga, more than 20,000 reinforcements poured into nearby Chattanooga, Tennessee over the course of only eleven days, all via the Northern railroad.

The system was not without challenges and controversy. When Federal officials grew weary of negotiating with private railroad companies to transport Northern troops—often at inflated rates—President Lincoln pushed a law through Congress that empowered the government to seize railways and imprison their owners if deemed necessary. The U.S. secretary of war was authorized to supervise the use of all railways as needed through a newly created agency called the United States Military Railroads.

Daniel McCallum, a civilian rail executive, was put in charge of the USMRR and given the army rank of colonel. Within a relatively short period of time, his efforts earned

him a promotion to brigadier general. At one point, McCallum kept railway crews working 24 hours a day to support a major Union military campaign, repairing damaged rail lines almost as quickly as Confederate raiders could wreck them.

Delivered by Rail: A Steady Flow of Troops, Equipment and Rations

McCallum was aided by a smart construction and operations manager, Herman Haupt, who came up with a way to keep the rails running with minimum government bureaucracy: Instead of using military manpower, Haupt simply installed civilians. The strategy was credited with allowing for a steady supply of Northern troops, equipment, horses, and rations into combat areas. At its peak, the USMRR shuttled more than 1,500 tons of supplies a day. The USMRR also developed wartime innovations, such as mobile rail-based artillery and rolling hospital cars. By war's end, the USMRR oversaw 419 locomotives, 6,330 railroad cars and 2,105 miles of track.

Brigadier General Daniel McCallum, a civilian prior to the war, ran the newly created military railroad agency.

Colonel Herman Haupt advocated for civilian manpower to run the railways.

ABOVE: Scores of rail trestles were built by the U.S. Military Railroads crews to move troops and supplies into position quickly, an important strategy for out-manning the South. ABOVE RIGHT: Railway crews repaired damage done by Confederates to tracks and bridges. The crew pictured here fixed a rail bridge across the Pamunkey River, bringing key support for General George McClellan in his invasion of Richmond. BOTTOM RIGHT: With the help of the USMRR, Federal forces were able to utilize mobile rail-based heavy artillery, such as the siege mortar pictured.

The War Changes Course at the Seven Days' Battles

ROBERT E. LEE SURPRISED UNION TROOPS AT RICHMOND
AND HUMILIATED A BRASH, YOUNG OFFICER.

I n the spring of 1862, nine months after their defeat at the Battle of Bull Run, Union forces again launched an offensive to capture the Confederate capital of Richmond. Leading the charge was George B. McClellan, a 35-year-old officer whom Lincoln installed as the army major general after the North's humiliating defeat at Bull Run.

McClellan, who replaced General Irvin McDowell, had scored a series of small victories in the mountains of western Virginia. He had a record as a superb military organizer and was seen by some as the savior of the Union. Northern newspapers hailed him as the "Young Napoleon." It was a point of view he seemed to share. "I seem to have become *the* power of the land," he confided to his wife, Nelly.

McClellan's spring offensive against Richmond was unusual: Instead of using the overland route and marching from the north, he put his giant 120,000-man

TOP: McClellan and his Army of the Potomac advanced on Richmond from the East in what became known as the Peninsula Campaign. ABOVE: The "Young Napoleon," General McClellan stood in uniform.

Army of the Potomac on troop transports, ferried them to the Virginia coast, then advanced on the capital from the east. By the end of May, McClellan and his army could see Richmond's church steeples. It appeared that the young general might capture the Southern capital, and perhaps even win the war. Then his strategy unraveled.

Robert E. Lee Takes Command

On May 31, 1862, General Joseph E. Johnston, commander of the Confederate forces defending Richmond, was seriously wounded at the Battle of Seven Pines. To replace him, President Jefferson Davis turned to his chief military advisor, General Robert E. Lee, who acted swiftly. Instead of waiting on McClellan's next move, Lee attacked. In what would become known as the Seven Days' Battles Lee launched a surprise offensive on June 25, 1862. His smaller army pummeled McClellan's forces in a series of battles.

Stunned, McClellan hurriedly put the Army of the Potomac back on troopships and steamed northward, blaming Lincoln and the secretary of war for the defeat. "If I save this army now . . . ," he telegraphed Washington, "I owe no thanks to you . . . ."

In just a single week, General Robert E. Lee rescued Richmond and reversed the course of the war in the East.

General Robert E. Lee took the offensive at the Seven Days' Battles and broke Union momentum.

Savage's Station on the Richmond & York River Railroad, pictured here on June 27, 1862, was the site of a Union hospital. On June 29, fighting broke out near the camp forcing the Union army to abandon supplies and the hospital with thousands of wounded still inside.

Unable to bear arms against his native state, Robert E. Lee left the Federal army to join the Confederacy after Virginia's secession from the North in 1861.

Robert E. Lee as an officer in the prewar U.S. Army, with his son Rooney.

Mary Anna Custis Lee with one of her seven children.

Robert E. Lee, the Confederacy's Great Hope

THE LOYAL VIRGINIAN CHOSE TO SIDE WITH HIS HOME STATE DESPITE PERSONAL BELIEFS.

Robert E. Lee was a Virginian with strong ties to the young nation. His father, Colonel "Light Horse Harry" Lee, had been one of George Washington's valued cavalry commanders during the Revolutionary War and a three-term governor of Virginia afterward.

Yet, when Lee was a toddler, his father fell deep into debt and was sent to prison. When released, Harry Lee tried to revive the family's fortune with land speculation in the Caribbean, but failed and died before he could return home. His widow moved young Robert E. Lee from the plantation where the family had lived into the city of Alexandria, so he could attend a free school.

As Robert Lee grew into manhood, he became determined to restore the family name. He distinguished

When the war began, Lee and his family were living in this home in Arlington, Virginia, which overlooked Washington, D.C. Federal forces confiscated the house and established a military cemetery on its grounds.

General Robert E. Lee and his favorite mount, Traveler.

himself at West Point, graduating in 1829 without a single demerit. He married Mary Anna Custis, the daughter of George Washington's adopted son, George Washington Parke Custis. When Mary inherited a plantation outside of Washington, D.C., the couple made a home there, eventually raising seven children together. During the Mexican-American War, he served as staff officer for General Winfield Scott, was decorated for valor, and was promoted to colonel. Afterward, Lee was appointed superintendent of West Point, which he strengthened academically. In 1855, he was made commander of the U.S. Second Cavalry in Texas.

I Never Desire Again to Draw My Sword.

On the eve of the Civil War, Lee was offered command of the Northern army. A devout Christian, Lee spent a long night pacing and praying over his options and then declined the position. He concluded that his first duty was to his home state of Virginia, even though he denounced secession as a "calamity" and viewed slavery as "a moral and political evil." He resigned his commission in the U.S. Army and vowed: "Save in the defense of my native state, I never desire again to draw my sword."

When Virginia seceded and was threatened by imminent invasion, Lee agreed to accept command of the state's troops, and when they were transferred to the Confederacy, he became a general in the Confederate army. During the first year of the war, he held various posts, eventually serving as the chief military advisor to President Davis in Richmond.

Lee's real military genius lay on the battlefield. An officer observed, "He will take more desperate chances, and take them quicker than any other general in this country, North or South. . . His name might be Audacity."

General Robert E. Lee, as he appeared when commanding
the Army of Northern Virginia.

Pea Ridge

Stones River

PEA RIDGE, PERRYVILLE AND STONES RIVER

In 1862, Northern forces steadily pushed back Southern armies in the war's Western Theater. In addition to victories at Forts Henry and Donelson, at the Battle of Shiloh and on the Mississippi from New Orleans to Memphis, Northern forces were successful at the battles of Pea Ridge in Arkansas and Perryville in Kentucky, and won an important strategic victory at year's end at the Battle of Stones River in Tennessee.

The officers and troops of the 41st New York Infantry at ease in the field. At the Second Battle of Bull Run, the regiment incurred more than a hundred casualties.

Lee's Maneuvering Produces a Major Southern Victory

SECOND BATTLE OF BULL RUN, AUGUST 28–30, 1862

General Robert E. Lee moved quickly to take advantage of his victory in the Seven Days' Battles.

While General McClellan and his defeated army were retreating to Washington, Lee moved his troops northward and attacked a garrison under Major General John Pope that was encamped at Manassas Junction on the old Bull Run battlefield. Pope was waiting to be joined by McClellan's army, but Lee did not intend to allow the two forces to merge. He reorganized his men into two corps, one under General Stonewall Jackson and the other under General Longstreet, and renamed the unit the Army of Northern Virginia.

On August 28, 1862, the Second Battle of Bull Run began as Lee attacked General Pope's forces. Jackson's men struck from the rear, while Longstreet led a devastating flank attack. Pope's army was routed, and—as at the First Battle of Bull Run—Union troops fled to Washington. In less than 90 days, Robert E. Lee had masterminded two victories in the Eastern Theater, undermining the North's gains in the West.

Wreckage of a bridge dammed up the Bull Run River outside of Manassas, Virginia. The Second Battle of Bull Run—just over a year after the first—was a discouraging loss for Union forces.

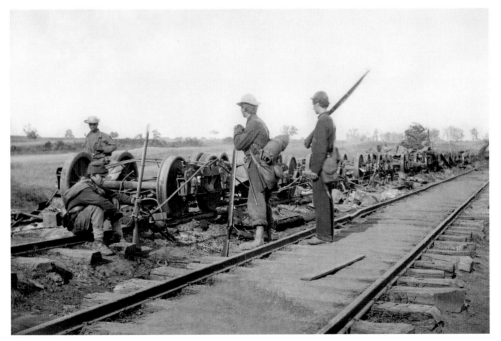

Demoralized Northern troops stood guard amid railroad wreckage near Manassas Junction following the Second Battle of Bull Run.

HEADQUARTERS IN THE SADDLE

When President Lincoln summoned Major General John Pope from the Western Theater to command Federal troops in northern Virginia, the general proclaimed in a speech that his headquarters would be "in the saddle." The statement prompted soldiers to joke that the general had confused his headquarters with his hindquarters.

Thomas J. "Stonewall" Jackson distinguished himself as an artillery officer in the Mexican-American War. In 1861, he served as a professor at the Virginia Military Academy.

In 1857, Jackson married Mary Anna Morrison, whose pastor father was president of Davidson College. The couple were devout Christians.

Shenandoah, 1862

GENERAL STONEWALL JACKSON DELIVERED ANOTHER
DECISIVE VICTORY FOR THE CONFEDERATES IN VIRGINIA.

In spring 1862, on the heels of a victory at the Battle of Bull Run, General Stonewall Jackson moved his army of men to Virginia's Shenandoah Valley with a new assignment: Prevent Federal reinforcements from reaching General George McClellan, who was rapidly advancing on Richmond.

The numerical odds were certainly against Jackson, who had been promoted to major general. He had just 17,000 troops, compared to McClellan's 52,000, and a 400-mile stretch of territory to defend.

But in a 38-day operation known as the Valley Campaign, Jackson marched his troops up and down the Shenandoah valley, fought six battles, defeated five Northern generals, and turned in victory after victory illustrating his maxim of warfare, "Always mystify, mislead and surprise the enemy if possible."

In some ways, Stonewall Jackson was an unlikely Confederate military leader. Orphaned as a child, he was raised by an uncle in the mountains of northwestern Virginia. He loved learning and was able to attend

General Stonewall Jackson's troops burned the bridge on the
Shenandoah River, June 4, 1862.

West Point only after a local student gave up his
appointment and the spot went to Jackson. Though
Jackson was largely unprepared for the academic rigors
of West Point, he was successful there and his motto
became, "You may be whatever you will resolve to be."

As a young artillery lieutenant in the Mexican-
American War, Jackson was cited for bravery in action
three times. After the war, Jackson did garrison duty
at army posts in the U.S., then joined the faculty at
Virginia Military Institute in Lexington, Virginia where
he taught mathematics. He was a devout Christian
and turned to his faith when his wife, Elinor Junkin,
died giving birth to their son. A year later, Jackson
remarried. His bride, Mary Anna Morrison, was the
daughter of a Presbyterian clergyman, just as his first
wife had been. In Lexington, Jackson flourished as
a family man, college professor, church leader and
Sunday school teacher for a class of slaves and black
freedmen.

Following the Shenandoah Valley campaign, Jackson
was summoned to a command post in Robert E. Lee's
army. There, Jackson would become Lee's "right arm."

In October of 1862, Jackson was promoted to lieutenant general and made a corps
commander in Lee's Army of Northern Virginia, where he became Lee's "right arm."

The War's Bloodiest Day

THE BATTLE OF ANTIETAM, SEPTEMBER 17, 1862

Despite his spectacular victories in Virginia, General Lee realized the Confederacy was steadily losing ground in the Western Theater. If the South was going to prevail, it had to win quickly, he believed: It was time for an invasion of the North.

Capitalizing on his recent victories, Lee led the Army of Northern Virginia northward into Maryland and toward Pennsylvania in September of 1862. He hoped the invasion would shake Northerners' morale, undermine support for Lincoln's war policies in the fall congressional elections, bolster his army with new recruits from Maryland, and threaten or capture Washington, D.C.

The invasion opened well for the South. Lee led his army northward and dispatched General Stonewall Jackson and a large portion of the army to capture a

LEFT: Northern troops advanced into combat in this illustration of the Battle of Antietam. More than 12,000 of them would be casualties by day's end. ABOVE: General Robert E. Lee's lost Order No.191 was found by Northern troops following Lee's route, revealing Confederate invasion plans.

Federal garrison at Harpers Ferry—which Jackson swiftly accomplished. Lee, meanwhile, led the rest of his army across the Potomac River into Maryland, positioning his advance to move either against Washington or into Pennsylvania. The invasion spread alarm throughout the North.

In Washington, President Lincoln urged General George B. McClellan, known for his caution, to quickly deploy the Army of the Potomac and block Lee's invasion northward.

Then fate intervened. As McClellan's army pursued Lee through Maryland, a group of his soldiers found an envelope containing three cigars wrapped in paper lying on the ground. Examining the wrapper, the men realized it was a copy of Robert E. Lee's official orders. It revealed both Lee's invasion plan and his troop deployments. The prize quickly made its way up the Northern chain of command until it reached McClellan. "Here is a paper with which if I cannot whip Bobbie Lee," he proclaimed, "I will be willing to go home."

When Lee realized that McClellan was bearing down on his stretched-out army, he issued orders to consolidate his forces before they could be attacked. But he was unable to fully do so by September 17, 1862, when the bulk of his men were overtaken by McClellan's larger army near Sharpsburg, Maryland at the Battle of Antietam.

Scores of Troops Fall

It would be the bloodiest day of the Civil War.

At Antietam, General McClellan had superior numbers and a strategic advantage, but his troops foundered. They were unable to break the right flank of Lee's army despite repeated attempts. More than 1,700 would fall in less than an hour trying to wrest a sunken wagon road, appropriately named "Bloody Lane," from the Confederate soliders.

Throughout the day, droves of troops from both sides were slaughtered at infamous battlefield sites such as the East Woods, the West Woods, Burnside Bridge, Dunker Church, and Miller's Cornfield. Lee lost more than 10,000 men—almost a quarter of his army—and McClellan lost more than 12,000. Six generals were killed or mortally wounded, and 12 were seriously injured.

Momentum ebbed and flowed for both sides, and late in the day, Confederate Major General A.P. Hill rushed reinforcements onto the field to relieve Lee's exhausted men. They were able to turn back a critical Federal assault and preserve Southern troops.

Though many consider Antietam to be a draw, strategically, the battle was a victory for the North. It ended Lee's invasion and seriously damaged his army; it also gave President Lincoln the victory he needed to issue the Emancipation Proclamation which declared an end to slavery. The order would not go into effect until 1863, and it had a limited immediate effect, but it transformed the Civil War, moving the central conflict beyond preservation of the Union, into a fight for freedom.

KEEPING COUNT

CAUSE OF DEATH: "OTHER"

Besides illness and battle, soldiers on both sides were killed by a variety of causes in the Civil War. U.S. Army records listed:

4,494
DROWNING

4,114
ACCIDENTS

520
MURDER

391
SUICIDE

313
SUNSTROKE

267
EXECUTION

2,043
OTHER CAUSES

In spite of the arrival of thousands of more Federal troops on September 18, General McClellan did not advance on General Lee's army at Antietam.

Northern artillery, such as this Pennsylvania battery, took a heavy toll on Lee's Southerners. Antietam was "Artillery hell," a Southern officer lamented.

BATTLE OF ANTIETAM, SEPTEMBER 17, 1862

In the span of 12 hours, in a relentless series of battles, nearly 23,000 men
were killed or wounded. This tactical map shows the battle's progression.

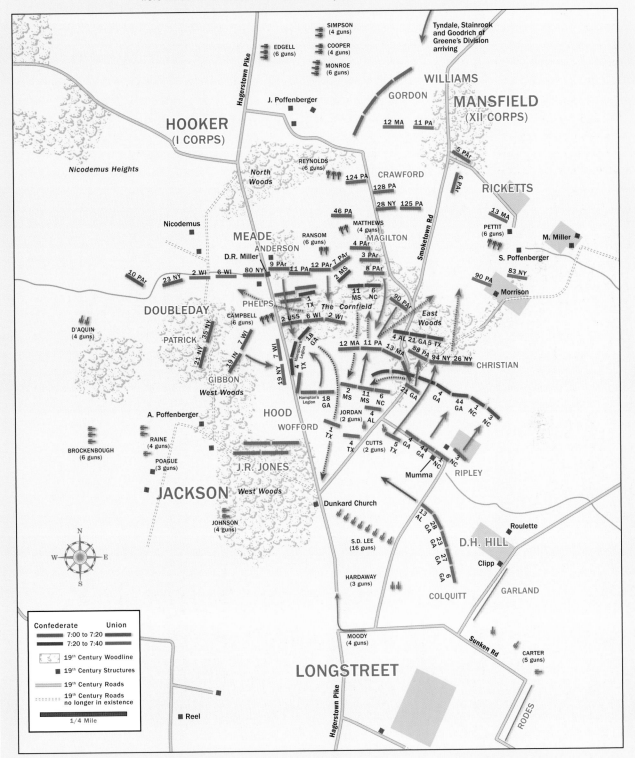

Confederate — Union
7:00 to 7:20
7:20 to 7:40
19th Century Woodline
19th Century Structures
19th Century Roads
19th Century Roads
no longer in existence
1/4 Mile

Confederate dead lay at their battle line alongside the Hagerstown at Antietam.

This postwar lithograph dramatically depicted Major General Ambrose E. Burnside's troops attempting to cross Antietam Creek on what became known as "Burnside Bridge."

Attempts by Northern troops to cross Antietam Creek were blocked by a small force of Southern riflemen.

WITNESS TO WAR

Saturated with Blood

AN EYEWITNESS ACCOUNT
FROM THE BATTLE OF ANTIETAM

Private Ezra E. Stickley, a soldier in the 5th Virginia Infantry, was a mounted aide to Colonel Andrew J. Grigsby, a brigade commander in Lee's army at the Battle of Antietam. Posted to the battlefield's bloody West Woods, Private Stickley was an eyewitness to Antietam's ferocious fighting until he was severely wounded. His account:

Soon after sunup the fearful battle began to rage. We first moved our artillery (Poague's Battery) to the front of our line to open the ball, and did so with good effect, exchanging a few rounds and then retiring behind the line. The spectacle now presented was one of splendor and magnificence. As the enemy advanced we beheld one of the most brilliant displays of troops we had ever seen. The Federals in apparent double battle line were moving toward us at charge bayonets, common time, and the sunbeams falling on their well-polished guns and bayonets gave a glamour and a show at once fearful and entrancing. . . . Just before this serious happening the command came to the troops all along our line: "Forward! Charge bayonets! Common time! March!" The command was obeyed cheerfully and with vigor, the men charging and firing as they went. But at a short distance they were halted by the powerful battle lines in front. They met at reasonably close range, and a battle royal was on, which continued through most of the day of September 17, 1862. . . .

About this time the Rochester Artillery, Colonel Reynolds commanding, stationed diagonally across Antietam Creek from us, opened a terrific fire, fixing their aim on the center of our brigade, where they could see the staff horses. I was then in the act of mounting my horse, a fine animal I had captured at Harpers Ferry. The first shell fell about one hundred and fifty yards behind our line, the second about seventy-five yards in the rear of the line, doing no damage. The third shell struck and killed my horse and, bursting, blew him to pieces, knocked me down, of course, and tore off my right arm, except for enough flesh to hold its weight. Seeing my horse about to fall on me, I jumped up and went straight to the brigade line of battle, where I was caught by two of our men and thus prevented from falling. I was saturated with blood, my right side from the blood of my own person and my left from the blood of my horse. Now, it was clear why I had lost my glove: I had no right hand on which to wear it.

Bodies littered a Confederate defensive line known as the "Sunken Lane."

A Federal burial detail took a break from its grim duty. At the end of fighting at Antietam, 3,650 Confederate soldiers had been killed; countless wounded died in the days and weeks following the battle.

Following the Battle of Antietam, President Lincoln removed
General George B. McClellan as commander of the Army of the Potomac.

Major General Ambrose E. Burnside, center, surrounded by his staff.

A New Commander for the North—and a New Disaster

A STAGGERING VICTORY AT THE BATTLE OF FREDERICKSBURG
ON DECEMBER 13, 1862 GAVE HOPE TO THE SOUTH.

In the weeks following Antietam, General George B. McClellan hung back. He did not pursue Lee's army and failed to launch a new offensive. President Lincoln, anxious to capitalize on the win, could barely contain his frustration. Finally, in early October, he journeyed from Washington to army headquarters in the field to confront McClellan personally. When the commander explained that the army's horses were too fatigued to engage, Lincoln was incensed. "Will you pardon me for asking what the horses of your army have done since the Battle of Antietam that fatigues anything?" he asked.

It was a fateful exchange. On November 7, 1862, Lincoln replaced McClellan with Major General Ambrose E. Burnside, an army corps commander from Rhode Island who quickly put the Army of the Potomac on the march. They side-stepped General Robert E. Lee and created a new line at Fredericksburg, Virginia.

General Burnside quickly moved the Army of the Potomac to Fredericksburg, Virginia, where he launched a disastrous attack on Lee's army.

The gains were short lived, however. Burnside lost time waiting for pontoon bridges to be built across the Rappahannock River. Once the Northern troops did cross over, they went on a looting spree. Lee used the extra time to fortify his line and soon the South's seven-mile-long line was almost impregnable. Open killing fields awaited Burnside and the men serving under him.

On December 13, 1862, a bitterly cold winter day, an unsuspecting Burnside attacked. It was a slaughter. Burnside had approximately 130,000 troops to Lee's 78,000 and ordered 14 shoulder-to-shoulder frontal assaults up the frozen slopes, but Lee's defensive lines were unbreakable. The Confederate infantry and artillery fire was overpowering. Watching the valiant enemy troops fall before his guns, Lee grimly remarked, "It is well that war is so terrible—we should grow too fond of it."

It was a shocking defeat for the North, which lost more than 12,600 troops, and for the South as well, which lost almost 5,300. Burnside attempted a fumbling follow-up campaign, but that too failed, and he soon was removed from the Army of the Potomac. As the gore-filled year of 1862 ended, a wave of hope spread across the South, while gloom enveloped the North.

Federal artillery pounded Lee's forces at Fredericksburg, but failed to prevent a bloody Northern defeat.

Working under a truce flag, Northern soldiers buried their dead within Confederate lines after the Union forces retreated.

5 THE WAR ON WATER

MANY NORTHERN MILITARY OPERATIONS RELIED ON THE SUPPORT OF THE UNITED STATES
NAVY AND THE CONFEDERATE FLEET, THOUGH SMALL, WAS ACTIVE AND INNOVATIVE.

Sailors aboard the ironclad warship USS *Lehigh*. This monitor-class ship was armed with a Dahlgren field piece, the most common cannon used during the Civil War.

"It was the most terrible storm of iron and lead that I have ever seen."

—A Confederate eyewitness to a Federal naval bombardment, 1865

Northern sailors aboard the USS *Wissahickon*. The 691-ton Federal gunboat served on the Mississippi, the Gulf Coast, and in the U.S. Navy's South Atlantic Blockading Squadron.

The North Builds a World-Class Navy

IN JUST FOUR YEARS, THE FEDERAL ARMADA GREW FROM ABOUT 50 SEAWORTHY SHIPS TO MORE THAN 600.

In 1861, the United States Navy consisted of approximately 1,400 officers, 7,700 enlisted men, and 96 ships—only about half of which were seaworthy. Lincoln immediately put the fleet into action, ordering it to blockade all Southern seaports, support joint army-navy operations, and protect the North's commercial shipping.

Four years later, the Federal armada would boast more than 51,000 men in uniform and 641 ships, including 60 ironclad warships.

As the war progressed, the U.S. Navy proved indispensable to Northern success. Equipped with newly built, state-of-the-art ironclad warships, the navy

supported army operations in important victories such as Forts Henry and Donelson, Island No. 10, Vicksburg, and Fort Fisher, and took the lead in capturing key Southern ports such as New Orleans, Memphis, and Mobile. Naval forces resupplied General William T. Sherman's army at Savannah after his March to the Sea, and over the course of the war, effectively blockaded more than three thousand miles of Confederate coastline.

The Northern naval blockade closed, bottled up, or helped capture every major seaport in the South— from Virginia to Texas—and effectively strangled the Confederacy. Naval warships also battled Confederate ironclads, and pursued Confederate raiders on the high

The USS *Cairo* waiting to dock in the Mississippi River. The ship would be the first ironclad to be sunk by a Confederate torpedo in December of 1862.

Federal sailors awaited orders aboard one of the U.S. Navy's mortar schooners. A 13-inch naval mortar could fire a 227-pound projectile over two miles.

seas. The North's eventual victory was due in great measure to the actions of the United States Navy.

"In all the watery margins, they have been present," said Lincoln. "Not only on the deep sea, the broad bay, the rapid river, but also up the narrow muddy bayou, and wherever the ground was a little damp, they have made their tracks."

Civil War Naval Operations

The Northern naval blockade closed, bottled up, or helped capture every major seaport in the South, from Virginia to Texas.

April 19, 1861 President Lincoln ordered the U.S. Navy to blockade Southern seaports.

March 9, 1862 CSS *Virginia* and USS *Monitor* engaged in the first battle between ironclad warships at Hampton Roads, Virginia.

April 7, 1862 Island No. 10, a key Confederate bastion on the Mississippi River, surrendered to Northern naval forces.

April 25, 1862 New Orleans, the South's largest city, surrendered to Northern naval forces.

June 6, 1862 Memphis surrendered to the North, virtually ending Confederate naval presence on the Mississippi River.

April 7, 1863 The Union suspended a naval attack on Charleston Harbor after just two hours.

July 4, 1863 Vicksburg was captured, giving Federal forces control of the Mississippi.

February 17, 1864 Warship USS *Housatonic*, attacked by the South's H.L. *Hunley*, became the first ship sunk by a submarine.

August 5, 1864 Northern naval forces captured the Gulf seaport of Mobile, Alabama.

January 15, 1865 Federal army-navy operation captured Fort Fisher, closing the Confederacy's last major seaport.

November 6, 1865 The Confederate cruiser CSS *Shenandoah* lowered its colors in Liverpool, England—the last Confederate surrender.

Timeline: 1861 | 1862 | 1863 | 1864 | 1865

An ironclad Confederate warship attacked Union vessels off the coast of Charleston, South Carolina in this period illustration.

The South Revolutionizes Naval Warfare

THE CONFEDERACY OVERCAME LIMITED INDUSTRIAL
RESOURCES TO BUILD OUT ITS FLEET.

When established in 1861, the Confederate States Navy existed more on paper than on water. Over the next four years, the Confederacy would buy, build, commission, capture, and otherwise float approximately 100 vessels of various types.

Although the C.S. Navy was tiny compared to its Union counterpart, at times it posed a serious threat to Federal maritime operations and to Northern commercial shipping. The fleet was led by more than 1,500 former U.S. naval officers who sided with the South and who were determined to defend Southern waters.

The C.S. fleet also had the advantage of a commander, Navy Secretary Stephen R. Mallory, who was focused on innovation. Under Mallory's leadership, the C.S. Navy constructed semisubmersible torpedo boats and launched the first submarine to sink a ship in combat. It also improved the technology for underwater sea mines—then known as torpedoes—and unleashed a bold offensive

against the North's shipping interests with a handful of high-seas commerce raiders.

Daring Attacks, But Failed Missions

The shoestring navy's effort was valiant and creative but achieved only mixed success. It launched powerful ironclads such as the *Virginia*, the *Albemarle*, the *Arkansas*, and the *Tennessee*. The CSS *Alabama* and CSS *Shenandoah* conducted daring attacks that harmed and alarmed Northern shipping. And the Confederate navy's technological innovations above and below water helped revolutionize modern naval warfare.

But at the same time, a third of its ironclads never saw action, and most of the others were sunk or scuttled. The commerce raids failed to cripple Northern shipping, and in the end, the Confederate States Navy was unable to break the Union's blockade of Southern ports or successfully defend the Southern coast.

Forced to create a navy from scratch, the Confederacy became an innovator in maritime warfare, including the development of sea mine technology.

The Confederate Torpedo Bureau led the way in developing technology for underwater sea mines—commonly called "torpedoes" during the war—and experimented with a variety of designs.

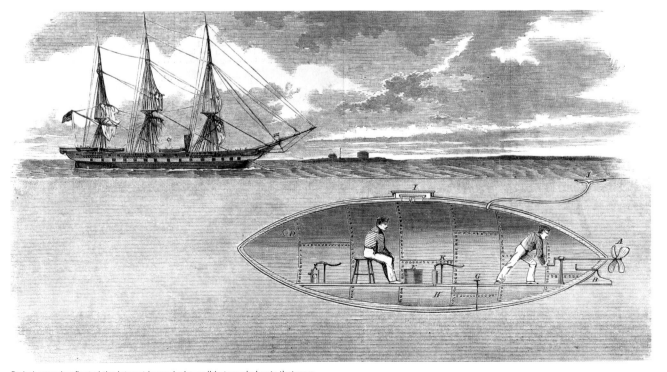

Period artwork reflected the interest in semisubmersible torpedo boats that were developed by the Confederate navy.

Gideon Welles was a strong supporter of the Republican party and held ardent antislavery views. He joined Lincoln's cabinet in 1860, before becoming Secretary of the navy.

Before he became a New England industrialist, U.S. Assistant Navy Secretary Gustavus V. Fox was a junior naval officer. As assistant navy secretary, he directed Federal naval operations for Secretary Welles.

U.S. Secretary of the Navy Gideon Welles

AN UNLIKELY LEADER BUILT THE NORTH'S FORMIDABLE MARITIME FORCES.

When Lincoln appointed Gideon Welles secretary of the U.S. Navy in 1861, he may have seemed an odd choice to some. A well-educated New Englander who wore a wig and nurtured bushy white whiskers, Welles was a former newspaper publisher and political operative. Formerly a Democrat, he switched to the Republican Party and helped Lincoln secure the party's presidential nomination at the 1860 Republican National Convention. Welles had no military experience—his civil service was limited to positions as a postmaster and state comptroller in Connecticut—but he *did* have a background in naval operations. During the Mexican-American War, he had competently headed the U.S. Navy's Bureau of Provisions and Clothing. He would eventually prove to be one of Lincoln's best cabinet selections.

A Well-Paired Team Leads the Way

As a leader of the U.S. Navy, Welles found a deft right hand in Assistant Navy Secretary Gustavus Fox.

They made a strong team. Welles was wise and experienced, and an admiring Abraham Lincoln jokingly referred to him as "Father Neptune." For his part, Fox was innovative and energetic. Together they oversaw the construction of state-of-the-art ironclad warships and upgraded the U.S. Naval Academy.

Welles and Fox were key in assisting the Union capture of one Southern seaport after another—a strategy that eventually strangled the Southern economy. They provided a strategy for an effective naval blockade, for critical support for army activities on inland waters, for aggressively pursuing Confederate commerce raiders, and for overwhelming the technologically advanced Confederate navy.

By war's end, the two men had not only led the U.S. Navy to victory, they had also modernized and expanded it to world-class stature.

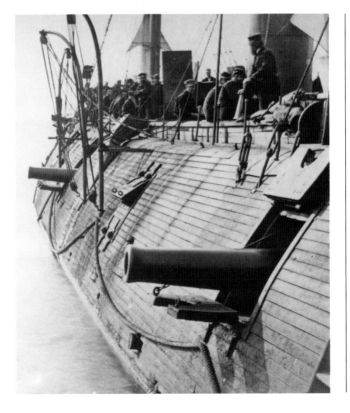

TOP: In addition to constructing new warships, like the ironclad USS *St. Louis* pictured above, center, the U.S. Navy also repurposed commercial ships like the USS *Tyler*, resting behind the *St. Louis* above, for warfare.

ABOVE LEFT: The USS *Essex* was originally a ferryboat called *New Era*. It was purchased by the U.S. Army in 1861 and fitted with iron armor before transfering to the U.S. Navy in 1862.

ABOVE RIGHT: Rear Admiral David Dixon Porter and his staff posed aboard the USS *Malvern*. A former Confederate blockade-runner, the steamer was captured by Union forces and became part of the blockade.

RIGHT: The USS *Galena*, one of the first Union ironclads, was considered a failure when it was pierced by Confederate gunfire at the Battle of Drewry's Bluff.

ARREST ON THE *TRENT*

In 1861, the Northern warship USS *San Jacinto* stopped the British mail steamer *Trent* on the open seas and arrested two of its passengers, James Mason and John Slidell, both Confederate diplomats to Great Britain. When Britain threatened war with the U.S., the Lincoln administration freed the two men.

As a U.S. senator for Florida, Stephen R. Mallory originally opposed secession, but nevertheless joined the Confederacy when his state left the Union.

C.S. Navy Secretary Stephen R. Mallory

A NAVAL VISIONARY TRANSFORMED THE SOUTHERN FLEET.

The South's most important naval resource was Stephen Mallory.

Born on the island of Trinidad and raised in Key West, Florida, Mallory grew up surrounded by water. Despite limited means, his widowed mother managed to put Mallory in a Northern boarding school for three years. The experience served as an ample educational foundation for Mallory, who did the rest on his own: By the time he was 38, he taught himself law under the direction of a local judge, became an attorney and specialized in maritime cases, was appointed collector of customs at Key West, and was elected to the U.S. Senate from Florida.

In the Senate, Mallory served as the influential chairman of the Senate Committee on Naval Affairs and was befriended by Mississippi senator Jefferson Davis. He opposed secession, but resigned from the U.S. Senate when Florida seceded.

Fighting Wood with Iron

The day after the Confederate congress created the C.S. Navy, President Jefferson Davis named Stephen R. Mallory as its head.

The strongest ship in the naval defense of Mobile Bay, the CSS *Tennessee* was captured by Union forces in August 1864.

Approximately 6,000 men served in the Confederate States Navy compared to more than 50,000 Union sailors.

The ironclad CSS *Virginia* was used not only for naval combat but to interfere with Northern shipping traffic.

Despite the South's lack of industry, Mallory believed the fledgling C.S. Navy should "fight wood with iron," and embarked on an aggressive upgrade campaign. He built a succession of ironclad warships like the CSS *Virginia* that rendered wooden warships obsolete. He improved sea mines and submarines and oversaw significant advances in naval artillery. He employed speedy vessels built in Europe to attack Northern shipping lanes.

Mallory's efforts rattled Union war planners and often sent the North scrambling to recover. But they were not enough to save the South. When the Confederacy collapsed, Mallory was arrested by Federal authorities and imprisoned without trial for almost a year. Upon his release, Mallory returned to his Florida law practice, but his health had deteriorated, and he died in 1873.

Built in France and commissioned by the Confederate navy in 1865, the CSS *Stonewall* did not reach American waters until war's end. Abandoned by its Confederate crew, it was confiscated by the U.S. Navy.

More than 17,000 African-Americans served in the U.S. Navy during the Civil War, and composed an estimated 20 percent of U.S. Navy personnel.

Black Sailors Take up Arms for the Union

AS NORTHERN SHIPS PROBED SOUTHERN COASTLINES AND RIVERS, SLAVES ESCAPED INTO U.S. NAVY CUSTODY AND JOINED THE SERVICE BY THE THOUSANDS.

It was Christmas Day of 1863, when the USS *Marblehead* came under attack near the mouth of South Carolina's Stono River. A Confederate shore battery raked the Federal warship with more than 20 rounds of scathing fire and killed the ship's powder boy.

Ignoring the deadly fire, seaman Robert Blake took over the dead boy's duties. He raced back and forth between the ship's magazine and its guns, carrying ammunition, and enabled the *Marblehead* to keep up a steady fire until the Confederate battery was silenced. For his valor, Blake was awarded the Congressional Medal of Honor. What made the award especially distinctive was his background: Robert Blake was an escaped slave.

Unlike the U.S. Army, the navy began accepting black crewmen as soon as the war began. As Northern ships probed Southern coastlines and rivers, slaves by the thousands escaped into U.S. Navy custody to join the service.

U.S. Navy secretary Gideon Welles approved the incoming flood of former slaves. He did not separate them into segregated units as the army would do later, but did require that the 17,000 black sailors be classified as ship's boys at the navy's lowest pay grade. By war's end more than 20 percent of the U.S. Navy's personnel was composed of black men in blue uniforms.

Officers and crew members of a Northern warship posed for a visiting photographer. At war's end, more than 51,000 men were serving in the Federal navy.

In 1863, the USS *Marblehead* was attached to the U.S. Navy's South Atlantic Blockading Squadron and patrolled the coast of South Carolina.

POWDER BOYS

Males as young as 12 served in the wartime U.S. Navy, often as the sailors responsible for keeping ships' guns supplied with powder charges during battle.

Federal warships patrolled the Southern coastline in search of blockade runners smuggling cargo in and out of the Confederate harbors.

Black Smoke and Moon Nights

RUNNING NAVAL BLOCKADES WAS A DANGEROUS BUSINESS, BUT IT
OFFERED SHIPPING COMPANIES POTENTIALLY HUGE PROFITS.

Immediately after the bombardment of Fort Sumter in 1861, President Lincoln ordered a blockade of Southern seaports.

The move served two purposes. It prevented the agricultural South, which did not possess the industry to wage war, from importing materials from abroad, especially from Great Britain. It also hampered the South's efforts to export cotton and other profitable crops that would finance a military build up.

Yet cordoning off the Confederacy's Atlantic and Gulf coasts was a herculean task. At the outset, the U.S. Navy struggled to patrol the 3,500 miles of Southern coastline with its nine major seaports and 189 harbors and inlets.

An Opporunity for Huge Profits

Despite its risks, running the naval blockade offered Southern and British shipping companies huge profits, and a specialized type of vessel was developed to

LEFT: Officers and crew of a darkened naval blockader prepared to pursue a distant Southern blockade-runner in this period illustration. RIGHT: The blockade runner *Colt* ran aground near Charleston. The wreckage is pictured above. When capture seemed certain, captains sometimes beached their ship so its cargo could be salvaged.

Textile industries abroad that relied on cotton from the South suffered when the U.S. Navy set up blockades in all Southern ports. Nevertheless countries like Britain and France officially remained neutral.

Some British ships, like the steamship *Dee* shown here, ran the Union blockade to move goods in and out of the South. These ships were operated by Confederate sympathizers and men looking to make a profit off cotton.

KEEPING COUNT

CIVIL WAR NAVAL BLOCKADES

AMOUNT OF SOUTHERN COASTLINE

3,500 MILES

NUMBER OF MAJOR SOUTHERN SEAPORTS

9

NUMBER OF SOUTHERN HARBORS AND INLETS

189

ESTIMATED NORTHERN BLOCKADERS DURING THE WAR

600

ESTIMATED SOUTHERN BLOCKADE-RUNNERS

300

APPROXIMATE NUMBER OF ATTEMPTS TO RUN THE BLOCKADE

1,300

SUCCESSFUL NUMBER OF BLOCKADE RUNS

1,000

A Federal soldier keeping watch for Confederate blockade runners.

evade capture by U.S. warships. A typical blockade-runner was a long, low, steamer that was camouflaged with lead-gray paint to blend in with the Atlantic seas. Collapsible masts and smokestacks reduced the ship's silhouette, canvas covers masked the noise of paddlewheels, and smokeless anthracite coal was used to eliminate the telltale plumes that could be spotted on the ocean horizon. Blockade-runners were designed to be fast, and to add speed during a chase, turpentine-soaked cotton bales or sides of bacon were shoved into the ship's furnace.

Sea captains who ran the blockade also developed specialized tactics. They would wait for a dark, moonless night, build up a full head of steam in the ship's boiler—then make a fast dash into the open sea, hoping to speed away from any patrolling Federal warships.

Outbound blockade-runners sailing from Southern seaports such as Wilmington, Savannah, or Mobile would carry cargoes of Southern cotton, tobacco, peanuts, or turpentine to ports in Great Britain via Nassau, Nova Scotia, or Bermuda. On the return voyage, they would bring back cargoes of English Enfield rifles, bayonets, percussion caps, bars of bullet lead, and uniforms. They also carried high-profit civilian goods that were scarce in the South. A profit of $150,000 earned from a single voyage was not unusual.

Fighting for the Lifeline of the Confederacy

The officers and crews of the Northern blockaders patrolling the Southern coastline could also earn sizeable profits—that is, if they captured a blockade-runner. The United States government auctioned off the cargoes confiscated from blockade-runners, and—as an incentive—split the profits with the officers and crews of the ship that made the capture. In 1864, for example, when the USS *Eolus* captured a blockade-runner, the captain earned $13,000, each sailor took home $1,000, and the ship's cabin boy received $500.

To the Confederacy, profits were almost secondary: The arms and equipment imported into the South by blockade-runners kept Southern armies in the field. By early 1865, blockade-runners had brought more than two hundred million dollars in war materiel and civilian goods into Southern ports, and exported more than 1.4 million bales of cotton to Britain. Blockade-running was the lifeline of the Confederacy.

The blockade runner *Robert E. Lee*, a 642-ton side-wheel steamer, made at least 20 successful voyages through the Northern naval blockade until captured by Federal warships in late 1863.

The specialized vessels that ran the Northern naval blockade were typically designed as fast, shallow-draught ships that could hug the shoreline. Many were camouflaged with slate-gray paint and fitted with collapsible smokestacks to reduce their silhouette on the ocean horizon.

RHETT BUTLER

Perhaps the most famous blockade-runner of all is a fictional one: Rhett Butler, hero of Margaret Mitchell's sprawling Civil War epic *Gone With the Wind*. Played by Clark Gable in the film version, Butler is a dashing, dangerous character who makes his living subverting the U.S. Navy. He only joins the Confederate army after the burning of Atlanta, when it is clear the South is doomed.

An 1862 illustration showed the USS *Cumberland* being raked by artillery fire from the ironclad
CSS *Virginia*. The Federal warship sank after being rammed by the *Virginia*.

The USS *Monitor* versus the CSS *Virginia*

NAVAL WARFARE WAS REVOLUTIONIZED IN A SINGLE DAY.

O n Saturday, March 8, 1862, just off the Virginia coast, a lookout for the USS *Cumberland* spotted an odd-looking vessel steadily approaching through the calm waters of Chesapeake Bay.

The *Cumberland* was part of a 20-boat Union fleet that boasted a total of 200 heavy guns—firepower that had convinced naval commanders they were safe from attack by anything the young Confederate States Navy might float. Yet, the strange-looking craft steaming toward the fleet was clearly flying Confederate colors; at 8:45 AM on Sunday morning, the *Cumberland* and the nearby USS *Congress* promptly opened fire.

Unknown to the Northern sailors, their target was the CSS *Virginia*, the Confederacy's first ironclad warship. The world's first battle between ironclad ships had begun.

Built on the Hull of the Merrimack

The *Virginia* had been constructed on the hull of the scuttled USS *Merrimack*, which Confederate troops had discovered in the abandoned ruins of the former U.S. Navy yard at Norfolk, Virginia. The 263-foot-long warship was armed with ten pieces of heavy artillery

Before joining the Confederate navy, Captain Franklin Buchannan, commander of the CSS *Virginia*, had run both the Washington D.C. Navy Yard and the U.S. Naval Academy.

and was covered with cast-iron plating to protect it from artillery fire. A 1,500-pound iron ram protruded from its bow beneath the water. The ship was commanded by 61-year-old Captain Franklin Buchanan, a former superintendent of the U.S. Naval Academy.

The Ironclad Takes the Day

The *Virginia* returned fire and tore a hole in the *Cumberland's* hull with its ram, sinking the ship and taking more than a hundred sailors with it. The *Virginia* then turned on the USS *Congress*, forced it aground in the shallows and set it ablaze. It wasn't until twilight approached that the *Virginia* finally steamed away. The ironclad's only serious loss was its commander: Captain Buchanan was wounded by Northern small-arms fire when he came topside to oversee the rescue of Southern sailors.

In contrast, Federal losses were shocking: two top-of-the-line warships were destroyed, three more had been driven aground, and almost 400 sailors and officers were dead, wounded, or missing. It was the worst defeat ever suffered by the U.S. Navy at the time. In Washington, D.C., news of the disaster sparked fear that the *Virginia* might steam up the Potomac River and bombard the capital.

The First Battle between Ironclad Warships

When the *Virginia* returned on Sunday, March 9, it expected to easily finish off the Federal fleet. Instead, as the ironclad moved through the Bay, it encountered a surprise: the USS *Monitor*, a Northern ironclad dispatched for its first mission.

Hurriedly constructed on orders of the U.S. Navy secretary Gideon Wells, the *Monitor* was described as a "cheesebox on a raft." It had a low, flat deck and like the *Virginia* was covered in thick, cast-iron plating. What distinguished the *Monitor* from the *Virginia* was its revolving, nine-foot turret, which was armed and could fire every two minutes.

The two ironclads circled each other at a range of about 50 yards, steadily trading fire and attempting to ram each other for hours, but to little effect. Artillery bounced off the hulls of both vessels. The course did not change until the *Virginia* struck the *Monitor's* pilot house, scattering debris that temporarily blinded its commander, 27-year-old Lieutenant John L. Worden. While Worden was being treated, the *Monitor* retreated and silenced its guns.

The first battle between ironclad warships thus ended in a tactical draw—but wooden warships were now obsolete, and naval warfare had changed forever.

This 19th-century illustration showed the CSS *Virginia* in drydock at Norfolk, Virginia's Gosport Navy Yard.

Lieutenant John L. Worden, the commander of the ironclad USS *Monitor*, was a seasoned naval officer who had once served aboard the USS *Cumberland*.

The crew of the USS *Monitor* relaxed on deck beside the ironclad's turret. On December 30, 1862, the ship sank at sea in a storm.

THE END OF THE *MONITOR*

Following its famous battle with the USS *Monitor*, the Confederate ironclad CSS *Virginia* was trapped by advancing Northern forces and was destroyed by its crew. Six months later, the *Monitor* sank in a storm off the coast of North Carolina.

At Hampton Roads, Virginia, the CSS *Virginia* and the USS *Monitor* engaged in history's first battle between ironclad warships on March 9, 1862.

WITNESS TO WAR

Aboard the CSS *Virginia*

LT. WOOD'S ACCOUNT OF THE BATTLE OF THE IRONCLADS

L ieutenant John Taylor Wood, a junior officer aboard the CSS *Virginia* during its duel with the USS *Monitor,* bore witness to the first battle between ironclads from inside the *Virginia.* An excerpt of his account:

After an early breakfast, we got under way and steamed out toward the enemy, opening fire from our bow pivot, and closing in to deliver our starboard broadside at short range, which was returned promptly from her 11-inch guns. Both vessels then turned and passed again still closer. The Monitor *was firing every seven or eight minutes, and nearly every shot struck. . . .*

Orders were given to concentrate our fire on the pilot-house, and with good result, as we afterward learned. More than two hours had passed, and we had made no impression on the enemy so far as we could discover, while our wounds were slight. Several times the Monitor *ceased firing, and we were in hopes she was disabled, but the revolution again of her turret and the heavy blows of her 11-inch shot on our sides soon undeceived us. . . .*

Lieutenant Jones now determined to run her down or board her. For nearly an hour we maneuvered for a position. . . . At last an opportunity offered. "Go ahead, full speed!" But before the ship gathered headway, the Monitor *turned, and our disabled ram only gave a glancing blow, effecting nothing. Again she came up on our quarter, her bow against our side, and at this distance fired twice. Both shots struck about half-way up the shield, abreast of the after pivot, and the impact forced the side in bodily two or three inches.*

All the crews of the aft guns were knocked over by the concussion, and bled from the nose or ears. Another shot at the same place would have penetrated. . . . At length, the Monitor *withdrew over the middle ground where we could not follow . . . We awaited her return for an hour; and at 2 o'clock p.m. steamed to Sewell's Point, and thence to the dockyard at Norfolk, our crew thoroughly worn out from the two days' fight.*

CIVIL WAR COMMANDO

LIEUTENANT COMMANDER WILLIAM B. CUSHING
1842–1874

If Lieutenant Commander William B. Cushing had been born a century later, he might have been a U.S. Navy SEAL.

A New York native, Cushing entered the U.S. Naval Academy at age 14, was appointed executive officer of a naval warship by age 19, and was the most famous junior officer in the U.S. Navy by age 20. He gained newspaper headlines by steaming into New York City's harbor with a captured blockade-runner, led numerous nighttime raids behind enemy lines, narrowly missed kidnapping a Confederate general from his headquarters, and helped lead a navy ground assault at the Battle of Fort Fisher.

Cushing's greatest feat occurred in 1864, when he led a behind-the-lines raid that sank the mighty Confederate ironclad CSS *Albemarle.* At war's end, he earned praise from President Lincoln and the official thanks of the U.S. Congress. But his exploits took their toll. Cushing lived his final years hospitalized with debilitating pain, where he died in 1874 at the age of 32.

THE CSS *ALABAMA*

The most famous and most successful of the Confederate cruisers, the CSS *Alabama* was a 1,050-ton, 220-foot, triple-masted sloop that was built under Confederate contract by a British shipyard.

Captained by Commander Raphael Semmes, the eight-gunned *Alabama* pursued Northern commercial shipping from Newfoundland to South Africa. From 1862 to 1864, the CSS *Alabama* captured more than 60 Northern merchant ships, burning almost all of them, causing a loss of more than six million dollars. It also fought and sank the USS *Hatteras* off the coast of Texas in 1863.

In June of 1864, the *Alabama* was sunk in a battle with the USS *Kearsarge* off the coast of Cherbourg, France. Semmes escaped capture and returned to the South, where he ended the war as a Confederate brigadier general.

The H.L. *Hunley* rested on a dock in Charleston, S.C., awaiting its fate as the first submarine to sink a ship in combat.

Submarine Warfare in the Civil War

THE H.L. *HUNLEY* BECAME THE FIRST SUBMARINE TO SINK A SHIP IN COMBAT.

Was it a porpoise? Or a log carried along by the tide? The watch officer aboard the USS *Housatonic* was unsure. It was the night of February 17, 1864, and the *Housatonic*, a 1,240-ton, 11-gun Northern warship, lay at anchor about five miles off the shore of Charleston, South Carolina.

As the unidentified shape closed in on the warship's starboard side, the deck officer realized the object was man-made and sounded the alarm. Guards on the *Housatonic* opened fire, but the strange craft rammed the warship's hull, causing a muffled explosion and a geyser of seawater on the starboard side. The *Housatonic* began listing, and within five minutes, had sunk in 28 feet of water, leaving most of its crew hanging on to its exposed masts and rigging.

Made from a Cylinder Boiler

The strange craft that sank the *Housatonic* was the H.L. *Hunley*, a Confederate submarine. Designed by Horace Lawson Hunley, the 40-foot vessel had been made from a cylinder boiler and could submerge fully thanks to diving planes and a hand-operated propeller shaft. A torpedo mounted on a spar that protruded from the *Hunley*'s bow was

On February 17, 1864, the USS *Housatonic* was attacked and sunk by the Confederate submarine H.L. *Hunley*.

designed to explode on impact. The *Hunley* carried a volunteer crew of eight sailors and a commander.

Despite its innovative design, the *Hunley* had a troubled history. In 1863, it had been shipped by rail to Charleston, where it was to be deployed to break the Northern naval blockade. On a test run, however, the submarine accidentally swamped, drowning five of its crew.

To boost confidence in his invention, Horace Hunley personally took it on another practice dive, but the sub failed to surface, and he was killed along with everyone else on board. It wasn't until early 1864 that the Confederate authorities agreed to try the *Hunley* again and find new volunteers to take the submarine into battle. This time, the crew under Lieutenant George E. Dixon kept the boat underwater for more than two and a half hours.

Soon afterward, the *Hunley* torpedoed the *Housatonic*. But for Dixon and his crew, it was a short-lived victory: The *Hunley* sunk outside Charleston Harbor, drowning all aboard. The boat remained lost until 1995, when it was discovered on the sea floor and raised five years later. The remains of its crew were ceremoniously buried in Charleston, and the craft was preserved in a special museum—as the historic forerunner of modern submarine warfare.

DAMN THE TORPEDOES! FULL SPEED AHEAD!

As the North's naval blockade reduced the flow of imported weapons and equipment into the Confederacy, Federal forces progressively attacked the Southern seaports that could not be effectively closed.

One of the last ports to fall was Mobile, Alabama, which was captured in August of 1864, when Admiral David G. Farragut forced his fleet of Federal warships past Mobile's formidable defenses.

Cautioned that Confederate water mines—torpedoes—lay in the path of his flagship, Farragut reportedly exclaimed, "Damn the Torpedoes! Full speed ahead!" The Northern victory at the Battle of Mobile Bay further isolated and weakened the Confederacy.

TALE OF TWO BEAUFORTS

Two small port cities with the same name—Beaufort, South Carolina and Beaufort, North Carolina—were captured in Federal joint army-navy operations early in the war and became refueling stations for the U.S. Navy's blockading squadrons.

The Battle for Fort Fisher—the Confederate Goliath

IT TOOK TWO MASSIVE ASSAULTS, BUT IN JANUARY 1865, THE UNION OVERCAME THE COASTAL
DEFENSE SYSTEM PROTECTING THE LAST SOUTHERN SEAPORT OF WILMINGTON, NORTH CAROLINA.

By late 1864, Federal forces had captured or effectively blockaded every major Southern seaport, except Wilmington, North Carolina. For Confederate General Robert E. Lee and his Army of Northern Virginia, it was critical to defend Wilmington so the South could receive military supplies.

Located 20 miles up the Cape Fear River from the Atlantic Ocean, Wilmington was protected by a massive defense system that was anchored by Fort Fisher—the largest coastal fortification in the Confederacy. The mighty fort stretched a mile and a half across and down a peninsula that overlooked the mouth of the Cape Fear River. It had been constructed under the command of Major General W.H.C. Whiting—one of the prewar U.S. Army's best military engineers—and was designed by his bright young protégé, Colonel William Lamb.

Fort Fisher, the largest earthen fortification in the Confederacy, protected the Atlantic entrance to Wilmington, North Carolina, which, by late 1864, was the South's only remaining major seaport.

Four Confederate soldiers stood in the battery at Fort Fisher. The unique fortress was built from earth instead of brick, and this enabled it to better withstand the shock of explosions.

Two massive U.S. Navy bombardments destroyed much of Fort Fisher's artillery in preparation for an assault by Northern infantry.

Rear Admiral David D. Porter, commander of the U.S. Navy's North Atlantic Blockading Squadron, unleashed the greatest naval bombardment of the war against Fort Fisher.

"I determined at once," Lamb would later recall, "to build a work of such magnitude that it could withstand the heaviest fire of any guns in the American navy." Fort Fisher bristled with heavy artillery—48 guns—and its defenses included a field of land mines that could be detonated by an electrical system.

In December of 1864, a joint Federal army-navy operation attempted to capture Fort Fisher and close the port of Wilmington. The assault started strongly, with Rear Admiral David D. Porter bombarding the

Major General Alfred H. Terry took command of Federal army operations against Fort Fisher after an unsuccessful attack on the fort in December of 1864.

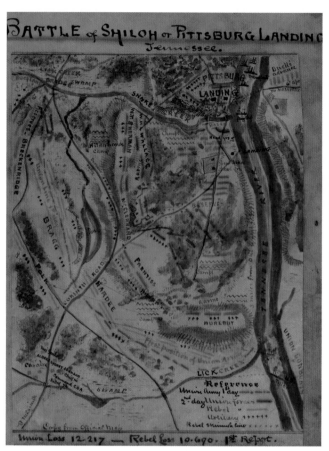

Fort Fisher was a giant, sprawling fortification that commanded the mouth of the Cape Fear River, shown here in a 19th-century map. Federal infantry assaulted it from the north.

Confederate behemoth, but army commander General Benjamin F. Butler recalled Northern troops from the Army of the James when they were just yards from striking due to the arrival of Confederate reinforcements. "Curses enough have been heaped on Butler's head," wrote a disgusted Northern soldier, "to sink him in the deepest hole of the bottomless pit." Without land troops for support, Admiral Porter suspended his naval maneuver and redirected his fleet back to the North.

The Lifeline of the Confederacy Is Severed

Dismayed by the army's retreat, President Lincoln removed General Butler from his post. In his place he installed General Alfred H. Terry, an experienced commander who had experience successfully assaulting seacoast fortifications.

In January of 1865, a larger joint army-navy force under General Terry and Admiral Porter returned to Fort Fisher with a fleet of 59 warships and approximately 9,000 troops from the Army of the James. For three days, the fleet's 627 guns pounded Fort Fisher, the largest naval assault of the Civil War. On January 15, General Terry sent in the infantry, supported by a group of volunteer sailors. Though the naval brigade quickly sustained casualties and turned back, the Federal infantry was able to scale the fort's high earthen walls and engage in fierce hand-to-hand combat.

The 1,900-man Confederate garrison defending the fortress was outnumbered and fought valiantly. Both Colonel Lamb and General Whiting were seriously wounded. But the effort could not keep Federal troops at bay. After six hours, Fort Fisher fell and Wilmington, North Carolina, the South's sole surviving seaport, was finally closed. After four years of unrelenting vigilance, the U.S. Navy's blockade of the Southern coastline had the Confederacy in a chokehold.

CSS SHENANDOAH

The Confederate cruiser CSS *Shenandoah,* captained by Commander James I. Waddell, was the only Confederate cruiser to sail around the world. Built in Britain, it raided Northern whaling fleets in the Pacific as far north as Alaska, and in December of 1865 became the last Confederate command to surrender.

TOP: On January 15, 1865, Northern infantry assaulted Fort Fisher, supported by a volunteer brigade of seamen. After hours of bloody hand-to-hand fighting, the fort's outnumbered garrison finally surrendered. BOTTOM: In a joint amphibious operation, thousands of Northern troops assaulted Fort Fisher, while the U.S. Navy pounded the giant fort with a sustained naval bombardment.

6 1863: THE TURNING POINT

IN THE WEST, NORTHERN FORCES OVERCAME SOUTHERN RESISTANCE. IN THE EAST,
THE SOUTH LAUNCHED AN INVASION. THE MOMENTUM CULMINATED AT THE BATTLE
OF GETTYSBURG.

The Civil War's greatest battle was waged on the sprawling fields of Gettysburg, Pennsylvania. Today, the site is a national military park.

"Oh, God! That I could see my mother."

—Last words of a dying soldier, 1863

By 1863, the war between the North and South had evolved into a war against slavery itself.

The Emancipation Proclamation Transforms the Northern War Effort

THE BATTLE FOR SOUTHERN INDEPENDENCE SPARKED A HISTORIC CRUSADE FOR CIVIL RIGHTS.

On January 1, 1863, President Abraham Lincoln's Emancipation Proclamation became law in the United States. After almost 187 years of Federal support, slavery was no longer protected by the Constitution.

Ironically, the Emancipation Proclamation did not actually free any slaves. Instead, it was a strategically calculated maneuver by Lincoln that declared slaves to be free only in areas of the South not occupied by Federal forces and allowed the practice to continue in areas controlled by Northern armies and in the border states.

The president had his reasons: He did not want to alienate border state slave owners who supported the Union, or disturb the peace in federally occupied areas of the South. He wanted to end slavery, but he also saw the proclamation as a tool of war that could undermine the Southern infrastructure. His chief aim of the war remained preservation of the Union. "If I could save the Union without freeing any slave, I would do it . . . ," he admitted.

Despite its limitations, the Emancipation Proclamation was a powerful blow against slavery, and Lincoln took an enormous risk in issuing it.

In the South, the majority of the population—even those who did not own slaves—viewed the proclamation as a Northern attempt to provoke a slave uprising. In the North, abolitionists believed it did too little. Union soldiers vowed they would not fight for Negroes and quit the army by the thousands. In Lincoln's home state of Illinois, the *Chicago Times* declared the proclamation a "monstrous usurpation, a criminal wrong, and an act of national suicide."

In New York City, fear of losing jobs to freed slaves led the city's Irish laborers—who also opposed a new draft law—to engage in a violent race riot, burning buildings in black neighborhoods and murdering black men in the streets. There was even concern within the Lincoln administration that the proclamation might provoke angry Northern Democrats to lead a secessionist movement in the Midwestern states of Ohio, Indiana, and Illinois.

Lincoln also lost important political support. Although the proclamation went into effect on New Year's Day of 1863, voters knew about it earlier. They registered their unhappiness in the November congressional elections, ousting legislators in Lincoln's Republican party. When Congress reconvened in 1863, the makeup of the House had shifted.

In the end, however, the Emancipation Proclamation gave Lincoln and the Northern war effort a major boost. It opened the U.S. Army to black troops, and African-American men surged into its ranks despite the army's segregated structure, ban on black commanders, and unequal pay for black troops. By war's end, more than 186,000 black Americans, most of them former slaves, had served in the Northern armies.

The proclamation also transformed the goals of the Northern combatants. Instead of fighting just to preserve the Union, Federal forces began to crusade for freedom. The North was able to claim the moral high ground and Abraham Lincoln was elevated to the "Great Emancipator."

Spurred by word-of-mouth reports of the Emancipation Proclamation, countless slaves fled Southern plantations to follow invading Northern forces.

The numerous slaves who escaped to follow Federal forces were officially designated as "contraband" by the U.S. government.

EMANCIPATION OF THE SLAVES.
Proclamed on the 22d September 1862, by ABRAHAM LINCOLN, President of the United States of North America.
Published by J. Waeschle, N° 162, North Third St. Philad.a

American slaves celebrated the Emancipation Proclamation, but it was opposed by Northern Democrats and cost Republicans seats in Congress.

1863

The South Begins to Retreat

Robert E. Lee's Northern invasion fell apart after the Battle of Gettysburg.

January 1 Emancipation Proclamation enacted, freeing slaves in Southern states.

May 1–4 Battle of Chancellorsville, the Confederate victory known as General Robert E. Lee's "perfect battle."

May 18 Federal siege of Vicksburg began, led by General Ulysses S. Grant.

July 1–3 Battle of Gettysburg, a pivotal moment for the North. Lee's Confederate troops retreated to Virginia.

July 4 Vicksburg surrendered, dividing the Confederacy.

August 17 Federal army–navy bombardment of Fort Sumter, which the Confederacy never surrendered.

September 9 Federal forces occupied Chattanooga, led by General Rosecrans and the Army of the Cumberland.

September 21 Rosencran's forces in Chattanooga were besieged by Confederate troops.

October 27 Federal forces managed to create a supply line through Confederate lines, refortifying the city and setting the stage for the final Battle of Chattanooga.

November 19 Lincoln delivers Gettysburg Address, considered to be one of the greatest speeches in American history.

November 23–25 Battle of Chattanooga; Federal victory paved the way for a Union invasion of the Deep South.

November 27–December 3 Confederate siege of Knoxville; Confederate General Longstreet, defeated by Union troops, retreated prior to the arrival of General William Sherman.

January
April
August
December

Confederate artillery made Vicksburg, Mississippi the South's greatest bastion on the Mississippi River—and Federal artillery helped pound it into submission.

Grant Launches an Attack on Vicksburg

NORTHERN FORCES ATTEMPTED TO CAPTURE
THE GIBRALTER OF THE CONFEDERACY.

By the spring of 1863, Northern forces had already captured both ends of the Mississippi River. But to finally split the Confederacy, Major General Ulysses S. Grant needed to capture Vicksburg, Mississippi, a Southern bulwark positioned on the mighty river between New Orleans, to the south, and Memphis, to the north.

Vicksburg was protected by a heavily armed bastion with artillery batteries that surveyed river traffic from 200-foot-high bluffs. The city's commander, Lieutenant General John C. Pemberton, was a native Pennsylvanian who had sided with the South. He was also a superb military engineer who had so fortified Vicksburg that it was referred to as the Gibraltar of the Confederacy.

After a fumbling, frustrating start, Grant directed a complicated offensive against Vicksburg in the spring and early summer of 1863. He advanced his 41,000-man Army of the Tennessee on a looping course through the Mississippi countryside, fighting a series of fierce battles along the way. By the time Grant reached Vicksburg, he was supported by naval forces and had increased his army to more than 70,000 troops. They were prepared for a prolonged siege.

A City Under Siege

Confederate president Jefferson Davis had ordered General Pemberton to "hold the city at all cost," and Vicksburg's Southern defenders stubbornly resisted the Federal onslaught. Yet they were no match for Grant's forces, and by the end of June, they were near starvation. So too was Vicksburg's civilian population, which was forced to live in hillside caves during the siege, surviving on mule meat and rats.

"Terror-stricken, we remained crouched in our cave,"

Besieged by Federal artillery, Vicksburg's civilians took shelter in hastily dug caves at what became known as "Prairie Dog Village." At times, Southern and Northern soldiers hid there as well.

AMERICA'S FIRST INCOME TAX

To finance the Northern war effort, the U.S. Congress implemented America's first income tax in 1861, introducing a 3 percent levy on anyone earning more than eight hundred dollars a year. In 1864, the rates were raised to ten percent on incomes of ten thousand dollars or more, 7 percent for five thousand to ten thousand dollars, and a 5 percent tax for anyone making from six hundred to five thousand dollars. The income tax was written so that it would expire in ten years. It wasn't until 1913, when the Sixteenth Amendment was passed, that a federal income tax would be reinstated.

In the South, the Confederate States Congress was hampered by tax restrictions in the C.S. Constitution, and could only enact a tax in kind, which required farmers, planters, and livestock growers to give a portion of their produce.

Confederate general John C. Pemberton, a Northerner by birth, oversaw Vicksburg's defenses.

Major General Ulysses S. Grant tenaciously attacked Vicksburg until its Southern defenders surrendered.

In order to collect taxes to finance the Northern war effort, President Lincoln's Secretary of the Treasury, Salmon P. Chase, established the Bureau of Internal Revenue, later known as the IRS.

a Vicksburg woman would later recall, "while shell after shell followed each other in quick succession. I endeavored by constant prayer to prepare myself for the sudden death I was almost certain awaited me."

Meanwhile, General Joseph E. Johnston, now in command of the Confederate Army of Tennessee, massed troops in hopes of rescuing Vicksburg, but nothing could save the besieged Mississippi bastion.

Following the Federal defeat at Fredericksburg, General Joseph Hooker was promoted to command of the Army of the Potomac.

Fighting Joe Takes Charge

A BRASH AND BRILLIANT MILITARY MIND, GENERAL JOSEPH HOOKER
BROUGHT BOLD FORCE TO THE FRONT.

No one who knew General Joseph Hooker accused him of being humble. When introduced to President Abraham Lincoln shortly after the Northern loss at the First Battle of Bull Run, he brashly informed the president, "I am a damn sight better general than you, Sir, had on that field."

A West Point graduate, Hooker had been decorated for bravery in the Mexican-American War, but fell on hard times afterward, living on the West Coast and "descending almost to the level of a beach-comber," according to one observer. Like Grant, Hooker saw the Civil War as an opportunity to restore his fortunes, and in the first two years of the war he rose from brigadier to major general.

He was a capable commander, even brilliant at times, but his enthusiasm for gambling, camp women, and whiskey raised questions about his character and discipline. Some even claimed that the name "hooker" was derived from the legion of prostitutes that he allowed to follow his command.

In January of 1863, Lincoln was casting about for a new army commander for the Army of the Potomac after its defeat at Fredericksburg. He settled on Hooker, even though the general had opined that the North needed a military dictator rather than a president. In his official letter appointing Hooker to army commander, Lincoln addressed the comment. "What I now ask of you," Lincoln wrote, "is military success, and I will risk the dictatorship."

Hooker earned national attention in the North as "Fighting Joe," a nickname that he acquired from a mistyped newspaper headline. Hooker lived up to the moniker. He was a bold, aggressive commander whose troops earned a reputation for ferocious fighting—and heavy casualties.

LEFT: Although bombastic and boastful, General Hooker was known as a competent commander. ABOVE: While commander of the Army of the Potomac, Hooker improved rations and medical care for Northern troops, but his relationships with his superiors were rocky.
BOTTOM: "Fighting Joe," seated second from the right, posed with staff officers.

Alfred R. Waud, a Northern combat artist working for *Harper's Weekly*, made this eyewitness sketch of the first day of fighting at the Battle of Chancellorsville.

Lee Outsmarts Hooker at Chancellorsville

CONFEDERATE FORCES TRIUMPHED AND THE NORTH
SUFFERED ANOTHER HUMILIATING DEFEAT.

In the spring of 1863, General Joseph Hooker launched a new offensive against General Robert E. Lee's army, which was in line around Fredericksburg, Virginia. The maneuver skillfully used the Army of the Potomac's superior numbers and caught Lee off guard with a three-pronged attack.

Hooker's main force moved against Lee's left flank at a crossroads called Chancellorsville; a second force attacked Lee's center at Fredericksburg; and a third force posted below Fredericksburg stood ready to crush Lee's army when it retreated.

"My plans are perfect," boasted Hooker, who had more than 130,000 troops to Lee's 60,000, "and when I start [to] carry them out, may God have mercy on General Lee, for I will have none."

When the battle began, however, it was Hooker—not Lee—who found himself needing mercy. As the Confederate cavalry under Major General J.E.B. Stuart probed enemy lines, they determined that the right flank of Hooker's army lay unprotected. They also discovered an unguarded, little-used wagon trail from which Lee's troops could make a surprise attack. To do so, Lee would have

Troops of the 110th Pennsylvania Infantry assemble near Fredericksburg on the eve of General Hooker's spring offensive. The regiment would suffer severe losses at Chancellorsville.

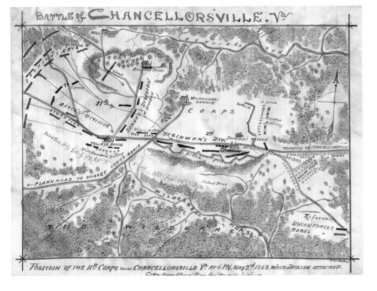

LEFT: A postwar map by a Northern veteran charts the battlefield action at Chancellorsville. RIGHT: The fighting at the Battle of Chancellorsville was so severe that it shredded entire sections of the Virginia forest.

During the fighting at Sunken Lane, in Fredericksburg, General Hooker's troops attacked the front and flank of Lee's army and suffered terrible losses.

to divide his men and risk having his troops destroyed piecemeal. Boldly, he decided to take the gamble.

Hooker Retreats

Lee ordered Lieutenant General Stonewall Jackson, who commanded a corps of his army, to lead a stealth attack on Hooker's right flank. On May 2, 1863, Lee advanced 15,000 troops to his front to divert Hooker's attention. Meanwhile, Jackson took 30,000 troops on a roundabout march through the woods to assault Hooker's right. Near twilight that day, Jackson's soldiers charged, screaming, from the forest thickets, surprising Hooker's troops as they sat around their campfires cooking supper.

The right flank of the Federal army collapsed in a panicky retreat, along with Hooker's "perfect" strategy. Another day of intense combat followed, but "Fighting Joe" could not recover. On May 5, he began withdrawing his forces. When President Lincoln received the news in Washington, he exclaimed, "My God! My God! What will the country say!"

Hooker put his army into lines north of Fredericksburg and waited on Lee's next move. The defeat at Chancellorsville "has shaken the confidence of the army," one of Hooker's subordinates said. Another described Hooker as the object of "universal disgust among the officers," while one critic called him "a used-up man."

Almost 155,000 troops fought at the Battle of Chancellorsville—more than 97,000 Northern troops and more than 57,000 Southerners.

LEE LOSES HIS "RIGHT ARM"

The Southern victory at Chancellorsville was General Robert E. Lee's greatest triumph, but it came at a devastating price. As General Stonewall Jackson and his staff reconnoitered in the darkness, they were mistaken for enemy cavalry, and Jackson was shot and seriously wounded by his own troops. In an attempt to save his life, Confederate surgeons amputated Jackson's mangled left limb. "He has lost his left arm," Lee lamented, "but I have lost my right."

As Jackson recuperated in a makeshift hospital ward at Guiney Station near Fredericksburg, he was joined by his wife, Mary Anna, who had recently given birth to their first child, a daughter. At first, Jackson seemed likely to recover, then he developed pneumonia. On May 10, 1863, the great Stonewall died. Said Lee: "I know not how to replace him."

More than 14,000 Federal troops and an estimated 10,000 Confederates were killed, wounded, captured, or declared missing at Chancellorsville.

In the summer of 1863, the south-central Pennsylvania town of Gettysburg would become the scene of the greatest—and bloodiest—battle of the Civil War.

Lee Moves North

FRESH FROM THE VICTORY IN CHANCELLORSVILLE, THE SOUTHERN ARMY MARCHED INTO PENNSYLVANIA WITH HOPES OF CAPTURING PHILADELPHIA OR HARRISBURG.

In late June 1863, the victorious soldiers of General Robert E. Lee's Army of Northern Virginia tramped along the dusty roads of southern Pennsylvania, 75,000 strong. It was an invasion of the North, and unlike the campaign that was halted by the Battle of Antietam the year before, this time Lee's army reached Pennsylvania.

Despite his spectacular victory at Chancellorsville, Lee believed that if the South did not triumph soon, it would not win at all. Northern victories in the Western Theater and along the Confederate coastline were slowly strangling the South, and it was just a matter of time, before the Confederacy would succumb to overwhelming Northern resources.

Lee advised President Jefferson Davis to move the fighting onto Union territory. The shift could benefit the Southern cause in several key ways. It could both provide relief for the residents of the war-ravaged state of Virginia and allow Lee to provision his army from the lush farmland of Pennsylvania. If Lee were victorious, he suspected the growing Southern threat would boost a Northern peace movement and that Union businesses would panic with war on their doorsteps.

What's more, Lee thought if he were able to capture Washington, Philadelphia, or the Pennsylvania capital of Harrisburg, he could earn the recognition of the Confederacy from Great Britain.

A victory on Northern soil could possibly lead to a negotiated truce, and produce Southern independence. Eventually President Davis agreed, and on June 3, 1863, Lee began moving his army northward.

THE INVASION OF PENNSYLVANIA—WORKING ON THE FORTIFICATIONS NEAR HARRISBURG, PA., JUNE 16TH, 1863.

Alarmed by the news of Lee's invasion, panicky Pennsylvanians began digging defensive earthworks outside the state capital of Harrisburg and as far away as Philadelphia.

Surprised by Lee's rapid march northward, General Hooker ordered the Army of the Potomac to break camp and pursue the Army of Northern Virginia.

BRANDY STATION

The Battle of Brandy Station, fought on June 9, 1863, was the largest cavalry battle of the Civil War and pitted Major General J.E.B. Stuart's Confederate cavalry against Northern horse soldiers under Brigadier General Alfred Pleasanton. Although the battle ended in a tactical Confederate victory, for the first time in the war, Northern cavalry proved equal to its Confederate counterparts.

In the spring of 1863, morale among Northern troops had waned.
Union fife and drum units were charged with boosting confidence.

A Soldier's Letter Home

DESPITE HIGHER NUMBERS AND BETTER SKILLS, NORTHERN
TROOPS WERE DEMORALIZED AFTER CHANCELLORSVILLE.

A s Lee's troops slipped out of their lines near
Fredericksburg; and headed northward, the 85,000-
man Army of the Potomac was encamped just a few
miles away on the other side of Virginia's Rappahannock
River. The army was superbly equipped, and its battle-
tested troops outnumbered Lee's forces—but many of
its soldiers were demoralized by their recent defeat at
Chancellorsville.

"We have got just enough men now to get licked,"
one observed, "especially if the officers get drunk every
time." Some Northern soldiers had come to believe that a
Southern victory was inevitable. Private John Sheahan of
Maine shared that sentiment in a letter home.

Camp Near Bell Plain
March 2nd, 1863

My Dear father:
As I have got a few moments to spare I will improve
them by writing you a few lines. . . . Does it look as tho'
the war is going to end by next fall? I think not. The south
are determined to have their Independence and they will
have it. And no soldier in the Army of the Potomac doubts
but what they will get it.

Some argue that they have not got the means to carry
on the war. But how did we carry on a war with England
the most powerful of European nations for seven long
years? We were fighting for our independence and we were
bound to have it cost what it may and we got it and so in
my opinion will they. I should be exceedingly sorry to see
our country divided and I do not think there is many more
willing to do more for their country than I am, but I am
almost inclined to think that we shall have to acknowledge
their independence.

I must write Mary a letter so I will close this. . . .
[John]

As Lee's Southern troops moved through the Pennsylvania countryside, Major General George Meade was appointed the latest commander of the Army of the Potomac.

In June of 1863, Northern soldiers in the Army of the Potomac had suffered recent losses and yearned for dependable leadership, but they were still determined to fight.

Major General George Meade Takes Command

THE ARMY OF THE POTOMAC WAS ONCE AGAIN ASSIGNED UNDER NEW LEADERSHIP.

When Lee's army headed northward toward Maryland and Pennsylvania, Union military planners were concerned. They urged General Joseph Hooker to pursue the Army of Northern Virginia, but instead the general peevishly tendered his resignation. President Lincoln accepted the offer, then dispatched an officer to inform the man who would be his replacement.

At 3:00 AM on June 28, Major General George Gordon Meade, a corps commander in the Army of the Potomac, was awakened in his tent with an important message: Meade was promoted to commander.

He would be the fourth officer to lead the Army of the Potomac in less than a year.

A balding, bewhiskered 47-year-old West Pointer, Meade had led troops in the Seminole and Mexican-American Wars, and commanded a brigade, a division, and a corps during the Civil War. Although occasionally irritable—one officer called him "a damned old goggle-eyed snapping turtle"—he was tested, disciplined, and competent. He was also from Pennsylvania, the Northern state now under invasion. "Meade will fight well on his own dunghill," Lincoln predicted.

Meade was a native of Pennsylvania—the target of Lee's invasion. In Lincoln's words, Meade would be determined to defend "his own dunghill."

Meade, seated in the center, was asleep in his tent when a messenger arrived to inform him of his promotion to army commander.

At Gettysburg, General Meade set up his field headquarters in this white-washed farmhouse just south of town.

At Gettysburg, Union general Meade would set up his field headquarters in this white-washed farmhouse just south of town.

When the Battle of Gettysburg erupted, Lee's army was spread across south-central Pennsylvania. The army's spearhead, under Lieutenant General Richard Ewell, was nearing the capital of Harrisburg.

Shots Ring Out at Gettysburg

UNION AND CONFEDERATE FORCES DESCENDED ON GETTYSBURG, AND FATEFUL DECISIONS SET THE COURSE FOR BATTLE.

In preparation for the campaign in Pennsylvania, Lee had reorganized the Army of Northern Virginia into three corps, which were now on the march through the south-central part of the state. The lead corps was nearing the capital of Harrisburg, prompting panicky civilians to flee, while state employees frantically packed up official records. Meanwhile, advance troops from Lieutenant General A. P. Hill's corps approached the town of Gettysburg.

By the morning of July 1, 1863, Lee's invasion was progressing just as he hoped, with one exception. Major General J.E.B. Stuart, Lee's flamboyant cavalry commander, had taken most of his horse soldiers on a raid around the rear of the Federal army. The maneuver left Lee without up-to-date intelligence reports, and his men had to move blindly through enemy territory at Gettysburg.

Both sides rushed troops to battle, engaging in major skirmishes on the west and north sides of town. After a brief pause to allow for reinforcements, the tide shifted in favor of the Southerners when

ABOVE: Confederate troops from Lieutenant General A.P. Hill's, 3rd Corps entered Gettysburg on the morning of July 1, 1863. An advance force from Meade's army was there waiting for them.

BELOW: On July 1, Federal cavalry from the Army of the Potomac took position on the outskirts of Gettysburg, awaiting the approach of the Confederate army.

GETTYSBURG CAMPAIGN

Confederate and Union troops converged on Gettysburg to engage in the deadliest battle in American history.

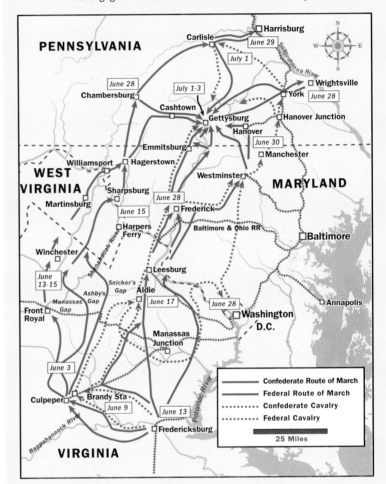

Confederate troops broke Federal lines. Northern troops streamed through Gettysburg in a disorderly retreat, and Lee appeared to have won a major victory on Northern soil.

A half mile south of town, however, the chastened Northerners were rallied by Major General Winfield S. Hancock, a commander of the Federal Second Corps, who redeployed them in a strong defensive line south of town along Cemetery Ridge. By the time the Union's General Meade arrived to take command that night, he found his army well positioned and ready to do battle again.

Federal general Winfield Scott Hancock, seated in the center, was known among the ranks as "Hancock the Superb." His actions at Gettysburg would reinforce this title.

Ferocious fighting marked the first day of battle at Gettysburg, where Confederate forces pushed up McPherson's Ridge west of town, breaking the Federal line.

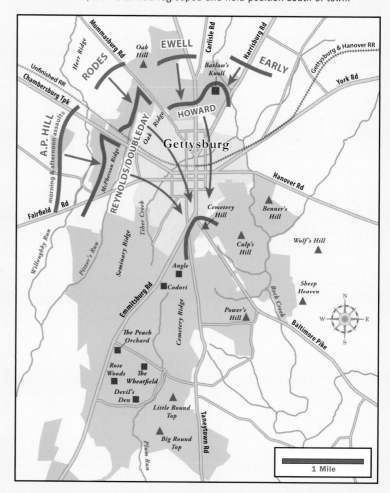

BATTLE OF GETTYSBURG

July 1, 1863—Day 1. Confederate forces initially broke through Federal lines and pushed Union soldiers into retreat through the town of Gettysburg. By nightfall, however, the North had regrouped and held position south of town.

At Gettysburg, Brigadier General John Buford deployed his Northern cavalry as infantry and ordered them to wait for the Confederate army. "You will have to fight like the Devil," Buford warned a subordinate.

GENERAL J.E.B. STUART

The Missing Eyes of Lee's Army

1833–1864

For critical battlefield intelligence, General Robert E. Lee looked to Major General James Ewell Brown Stuart, who commanded the Army of Northern Virginia's cavalry division. Called Jeb, for his initials, the 30-year-old Stuart was a red-bearded West Pointer who had fought Indians in prewar Kansas and quickly gained rank in Confederate service. Daring and flamboyant, Stuart favored thigh-high cavalry boots, a red-lined cape, a yellow sash, and a plumed hat. Twice in 1862, he led the Confederate cavalry entirely around the Army of the Potomac; he also distinguished himself as a commander at the battles of Second Bull Run and Chancellorsville.

Lee valued Stuart's abilities and looked upon him in an almost fatherly manner. "I can scarcely think of him without weeping," he would comment after Stuart was killed in action in 1864.

On the eve of Lee's invasion of Pennsylvania, however, Stuart had been surprised by Federal cavalry at the Battle of Brandy Station. Perhaps in an attempt to restore his reputation—or because he misunderstood Lee's orders—Stuart led his cavalry on a wide-ranging raid far from Lee's army during the march to Gettysburg. The lack of cavalry deprived Lee of vital reconnaissance, and left his army to move blindly through enemy territory.

U.S. major general Winfield Scott Hancock was an experienced officer whose decisive action on Gettysburg's first day stopped a Federal panic.

Little Round Top, on the left, and Big Round Top, to the right, anchored the southern end of the Federal left flank on Cemetery Ridge. Little Round Top offered a strategic advantage to whichever army successfully occupied it.

Battle Lines Are Drawn

SOLDIERS FROM BOTH SIDES STRETCHED AROUND
GETTYSBURG IN A TEST OF STRATEGY AND STRENGTH.

By midday on July 2, General Meade had deployed his troops in a battle line extending south from Gettysburg. It curved around Culp's Hill, a rocky, wooded knob on the edge of town, and around nearby Cemetery Hill. From there, it stretched southward along Cemetery Ridge for more than a mile to the base of two wooded hills—Little Round Top and Big Round Top.

While setting his line, Meade and his chief engineer, Major General Gouverneur K. Warren, recognized the strategic importance of placing artillery on Little Round Top, and hurriedly sent troops to seize it. The defensive move was designed to prevent Southerners from taking Little Round Top and to preserve the Northern line.

Lee meanwhile deployed his army along Seminary Ridge and through the edge of town. General James Longstreet, commander of Lee's First Corps, reportedly urged Lee to take a defensive position, but Lee was confident that his troops could make a successful attack.

"No," Lee said, "the enemy is there, and I am going to attack him there." Lee ordered Longstreet to direct simultaneous Confederate assaults on both ends of the Federal line—and to do so quickly. Longstreet, however, was disgruntled with Lee's plans and did not launch the Confederate attack until late afternoon.

The Federal Line Holds

Lee's troops smashed against the Federal line and almost turned it on both flanks—a move which could have ended the battle, and perhaps the war, in a Southern victory. The Southerners also pierced the Federal line near its center.

But the Union forces rallied with unexpected strength. On the Federal far-left flank, the 20th Maine Infantry turned back a Confederate attack on Little Round Top. On Culp's Hill, an equally heroic stand by the 137th New York Infantry blocked Southern forces. The 1st Minnesota Infantry suffered grievous loss of life, but plugged the break in the center of the Federal line. Despite a bloody battering, at the end of the battle's second day, the Federal line stood firm.

Culp's Hill, on the northern end of the Federal line at Gettysburg, was the scene of savage fighting on July 2, as Confederate troops repeatedly attempted to turn the Federal right flank.

Brigadier General Gouverneur K. Warren rushed Northern troops to hold Little Round Top, preventing Southern troops from putting artillery atop it.

LIEUTENANT GENERAL JAMES LONGSTREET

1921–1904

Known as "Old Pete," James Longstreet was one of the Confederacy's most distinguished commanders. Born in South Carolina, Longstreet was a veteran of the Mexican-American War where he served in the 8th Infantry. While he was one of General Lee's most trusted men—Lee called him "my old war horse"—Longstreet criticized Lee's battle tactics after the war, which made him a controversial figure in the South.

BATTLE OF GETTYSBURG

July 2, 1863—Day 2. Now south of town, Union forces reassembled for battle. The Confederates fought ferociously and made some inroads, but overall the Federal line held.

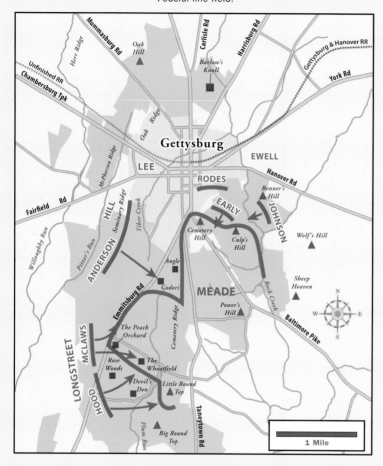

At a critical moment on Gettysburg's second day, Colonel William Colvill and the 1st Minnesota Infantry saved the Federal line from breaking. Of 262 troops, only 47 of the Minnesotans survived.

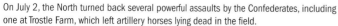
On July 2, the North turned back several powerful assaults by the Confederates, including one at Trostle Farm, which left artillery horses lying dead in the field.

Confederate troops, shot down in the second day's fighting at Gettysburg, awaited burial on the edge of the battlefield's blood-soaked Peach Orchard.

The 20th Maine Infantry made a bold bayonet charge down Little Round Top's boulder-strewn slope, driving back an assault by Lee's army.

THE KILLER ANGELS

The Battle of Gettysburg is immortalized in Michael Shaara's 1975 Pulitzer Prize winning–novel *The Killer Angels*. Using real characters such as Generals Robert E. Lee, Joshua Lawrence Chamberlain, and James Longstreet to tell the story, Shaara captures the emotional lead up to battle and the three bloody days of fighting. Hailed as one of the most accurate accounts of war in fiction, the novel was the basis for the 1993 film *Gettysburg*.

Colonel Joshua Lawrence Chamberlain, commander of the 20th Maine Infantry, was a former college professor and theologian, and not a professional soldier. He *was* a natural leader, however, and led his regiment in a successful defense of the Federal far left flank at Little Round Top.

Colonel William C. Oates led the 15th Alabama Infantry in repeated assaults against the 20th Maine. The Alabamians, however, could not overwhelm the men from Maine.

The assault against the 20th Maine was led by troops of the 15th Alabama Infantry, who had to scale Big Round Top, in the distance, before they could make their attack.

THE FACES OF WAR

The Battle of Wills on Little Round Top

TWO BRAVE AND DETERMINED COMMANDERS FACED OFF
IN A PIVOTAL FIGHT AT GETTYSBURG.

Colonel Joshua Chamberlain:
The Professor

When Lee's army struck Little Round Top on July 2, the Federal far-left flank was defended by the 20th Maine Infantry under Colonel Joshua Chamberlain. "I place you here!" Chamberlain's superior officer told him. "You are to hold this ground at all costs."

The 34-year-old Chamberlain was a college professor, not a professional soldier. A devout Christian, he taught classes in "revealed and natural religion" at Maine's Bowdoin College and was fluent in ten languages. Mild-mannered and disciplined, Chamberlain was a natural leader who had joined the army instead of taking a paid sabbatical to Europe. He and the 20th Maine underwent a bloody baptism of fire at Fredericksburg; at Little Round Top they stubbornly turned back repeated assaults by some of Lee's best troops.

For his leadership at Gettysburg, Chamberlain was awarded the Congressional Medal of Honor. After the war, he ran as a Republican and was elected governor of Maine.

Colonel William Oates: The Runaway

Spearheading the assault on Chamberlain's position on Little Round Top was the 15th Alabama Infantry, commanded by Colonel William C. Oates.

Raised in a poor farming family in southeastern Alabama, Oates received little formal education as a child, and fled Alabama after a brush with the law at age 16. He worked as a house painter, deckhand, and gambler until he cobbled together enough money to attend school. He later became a teacher, and then a lawyer, and newspaper editor.

When the war began, Oates raised his own infantry company, saw combat in Stonewall Jackson's Shenandoah Valley Campaign, and was made colonel and commander of the 15th Alabama Infantry by age 28. The regiment started July 2 marching 25 miles that day, but when Oates was ordered to assault the Federal far-left flank at Little Round Top, he obeyed.

"With a withering and deadly fire pouring in upon us from every direction," he would later recount, "it seemed that the entire command was doomed to destruction." The exhausted Alabamians finally retreated when Chamberlain and his troops—almost out of ammunition—struck them with a bayonet counterattack.

Later in the war Oates would survive a near-fatal wound. Like Chamberlain, he entered politics and in 1894 was elected governor of Alabama.

The High-Water Mark

GENERAL MEADE ACCURATELY PREDICTED THAT CONFEDERATE FORCES WOULD ATTACK HIS LINE AT THE MIDDLE.
THOUGH THE REBEL CHARGE WAS IMPRESSIVE, IT WAS TURNED BACK BY WELL-PREPARED FEDERAL TROOPS.

The next morning, Friday, July 3, 1863, General Lee planned to resume his attack on the Federal flanks, believing the Union troops there were near the point of breaking. However, General Longstreet—Lee's second-in-command—was again slow to get the Southern troops in place. So Lee changed his battle plan: He would attack the middle of the Federal line.

As a ploy to divert Federal troops, Lee started by dispatching General J.E.B. Stuart and his cavalry, which had finally arrived from their raid, to assault the Federal

BATTLE OF GETTYSBURG

July 3, 1863—Day 3. A bold Southern attack on the center of the North's line was met with extra troops and artillery, as well as heavy casualties. Lee was forced to retreat into Virginia.

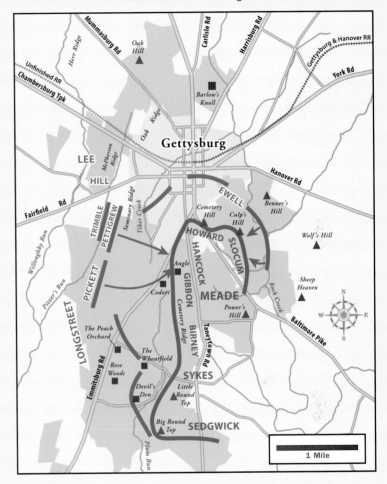

LEFT: Federal artillery crews poured fire into the distant Confederate ranks as the Pickett-Pettigrew Charge advanced toward the Federal line on Cemetery Ridge, depicted in this painting. The Federal artillery and infantry fire was described as "murderous—too much for human valor."

rear. Lee then proceeded with a massive artillery bombardment of the Federal line on Cemetery Ridge. Starting at 1:00 PM, it seemed as if "the whole Rebel line was pouring out thunder and iron," a Northern officer would recall.

More than 170 pieces of Confederate field artillery pounded the Federal line, but bombardment was largely sound and fury—most of it overshot the Federal line and did minimal damage.

At about 3 PM, more than 13,000 Southern troops emerged from the distant woods opposite Cemetery Ridge and began advancing toward the Federal line under fluttering red battle flags, as if on parade. On the right was Major General George E. Pickett's division of Longstreet's corps, and on the left was Brigadier General James J. Pettigrew's division, supported by two other brigades. They advanced resolutely over more than three-quarters of a mile of open fields. "It was a magnificent line of battle," a Northern officer would later admit. "[It] looked like a stream or river of silver moving toward us."

CIVIL WAR STATS:
THE HUMAN COST OF BATTLE AT GETTYSBURG

	FEDERAL	CONFEDERATE
DEAD	3,155	3,903
WOUNDED	4,529	18,735
MISSING	5,365	5,425
TOTAL	23,049	28,063

A surgeon embalms the body of a fallen soldier.

Federal troops wounded in the Battle of Chancellorsville convalesce.

Brigadier General Alexander Hays commanded the Federal troops facing Pettigrew's advancing Confederates. As the Southerners approached, Hays yelled to his men, "Now, boys, you'll see some fun!"

Staggering Losses

The Federal army was ready. During the night, General Meade polled his senior commanders, asking if they thought the army should be withdrawn to do battle elsewhere. "Stay and fight it out," they advised him. Meade agreed—and predicted that Lee would next strike the center of the Federal line.

Accordingly, he shifted troops to the center of his line, which was supported by well-placed artillery. As a huge mass of Southern soldiers advanced across the fields under fluttering flags, they were decimated by Federal artillery fire. "Arms, heads, blankets, guns, and knapsacks were thrown and tossed into the air," an Ohio soldier grimly observed.

It was a similar scene wherever Confederates breached the Federal line. When they reached the top of Cemetery Ridge, they were brought down by volley fire that one New Jersey soldier described as "a slaughter pen." Reduced to almost half their numbers, the bloodied survivors streamed to the Confederate rear. There they were met by Lee on horseback, who rode among them, saying repeatedly, "It's all my fault. It's all my fault."

General Pickett, mounted, received permission from General Longstreet to lead off the Pickett-Pettigrew Charge. Although placed in command of the attack by General Lee, Longstreet obeyed orders reluctantly.

GENERAL JAMES JOHNSTON PETTIGREW
1825–1875

A professor at the Naval Observatory, James Johnston Pettigrew had no combat training or field experience before the war. He initially resisted command by enlisting in the Confederate army as a private, only to be rapidly promoted.

GENERAL GEORGE E. PICKETT
1828–1863

By contrast, George E. Pickett was an experienced soldier, having earned two promotions in the Mexican-American War. He nonetheless carried the dubious distinction of finishing last in his West Point class. The charge he led at Gettysburg with Pettigrew ended disasterously.

On the Northern side, when General Meade was assured that his army had won, he looked surprised, and simply muttered, "Thank God."

The face-off at Gettysburg between the troops of General George Pickett and those of James Pettigrew was the last time the South came close to winning the war and would become known as the "High-Water Mark of the Confederacy."

Gettysburg was the largest battle ever fought on the North American continent. More than 51,000 troops were killed, wounded, or missing— approximately 28,000 Confederates and 23,000 Federals.

After waiting a day for a Federal follow-up attack that never came, General Lee led his defeated army back to Virginia. Horrible, bloody fighting would continue for almost two more years, but the Battle of Gettysburg marked the beginning of the end of the Civil War.

A crowd of 15,000 gathered before President Lincoln's Gettysburg Address on November 19, 1863.

The Gettysburg Address

A SPEECH THAT ALMOST DIDN'T HAPPEN BECAME
ONE OF THE MOST HERALDED IN AMERICAN HISTORY.

On November 19, 1863, Abraham Lincoln delivered his famous Gettysburg Address—but he was not the main speaker. The event was the dedication of a new cemetery for the Northern dead at Gettysburg, and the ceremony's organizers had invited famed orator Edward Everett to rally the crowd. As an apparent afterthought, the president was included to make "a few appropriate remarks" and given second billing.

The day he left Washington, Lincoln almost canceled his appearance because his young son, Tad, had fallen seriously ill, and his wife Mary was fearful. But the president proceeded with his plans and, upon arriving at Gettysburg, was relieved to learn that Tad's condition had improved.

An estimated 15,000 spectators attended the gathering and listened as Everett delivered a rousing two-hour patriotic speech. Lincoln followed, and spoke for two minutes: The Gettysburg Address consisted of 272 words. When he finished, the audience was subdued. Lincoln sat down, appearing dejected, and muttered to a colleague, "that speech won't scour."

When a transcript appeared in Northern newspapers, however, the public response was enthusiastic—and over time the acclaim increased. Lincoln's stirring words—that "this nation, under God, shall have a new birth of freedom . . . and that government of the people, by the people and for the people, shall not perish from the earth" would ring through the ages as an inspiration for all Americans.

Address delivered at the dedication of the cemetery at Gettysburg.

Four score and seven years ago our fathers brought forth on this continent, a new nation, conceived in Liberty, and dedicated to the proposition that all men are created equal.

Now we are engaged in a great civil war, testing whether that nation, or any nation so conceived and so dedicated, can long endure. We are met on a great battlefield of that war. We have come to dedicate a portion of that field, as a final resting place for those who here gave their lives that that nation might live. It is altogether fitting and proper that we should do this.

But, in a larger sense, we can not dedicate—we can not consecrate—we can not hallow—this ground. The brave men, living and dead, who struggled here have consecrated it, far above our poor power to add or detract. The world will little note, nor long remember what we say here, but it can never forget what they did here. It is for us the living, rather, to be dedicated here to the unfinished work which they who fought here have thus far so nobly advanced. It is rather for us to be here dedicated to the great task remaining before us—that from these honored dead we take increased devotion to that cause for which they gave the last full measure of devotion—that we here highly resolve that these dead shall not have died in vain—that this nation, under God, shall have a new birth of freedom—and that government of the people, by the people, for the people, shall not perish from the earth.

Abraham Lincoln.

November 19, 1863.

Lincoln wrote several drafts of his Gettysburg Address. The audience initially reacted with stunned silence, prompting Lincoln to conclude, "that speech won't scour." Instead, it would become one of the most famous addresses in American history.

Today, the site where Lincoln delivered the Gettysburg Address is marked by a memorial.

NO TRIAL FOR PRISONERS

During the Civil War, Lincoln stirred controversy by suspending habeas corpus, which guaranteed a prisoner the right to a trial. As many as 20,000 Americans were imprisoned without trial for opposing administration policy, but Lincoln defended his actions as a wartime necessity.

As depicted in this 1863 newspaper image, General Grant, left, met with Confederate General Pemberton to arrange Vicksburg's surrender. Pemberton, who knew Grant from the Mexican-American War, hoped to gain good terms by surrendering on the Fourth of July.

Private W.P. Ward served in the 40th Georgia Infantry, which was engaged in the defense of Vicksburg until forced to surrender.

Private Charles "Charlie" Judkins of the 9th New Hampshire Infantry. His regiment was among the victorious Federal troops who captured Vicksburg.

During the siege of Vicksburg, Federal troops repeatedly assaulted the Confederate defenses—
sometimes with disastrous results. "We [were] shot down like dogs," one Northern solder reported.

Vicksburg Surrenders to Northern Forces

DOUBLE DEFEATS LEFT THE CONFEDERATE
FORCES REELING.

On July 4, 1863—the day after the South's decisive loss at Gettysburg—Confederate troops surrendered the vitally important stronghold of Vicksburg, Mississippi. It had been a harrowing 47-day siege by Northern forces under General Ulysses S. Grant, and Vicksburg's defenders could take no more. They had lost 30,000 troops, 60,000 small arms, 172 cannons, and suffered a huge blow to morale.

By capitulating to the North on Independence Day, Lieutenant General John C. Pemberton, Vicksburg's Confederate commander, hoped to get better terms. But when he met with Grant, the Union general was firm. He would take nothing less than unconditional surrender.

The victory, which split the South and enabled Northern forces to finally seize control of the Mississippi River, lionized Grant in the North. "The Father of Waters," proclaimed Abraham Lincoln, "again goes unvexed to the sea."

THE RICHMOND BREAD RIOT

By 1863, the Confederate capital of Richmond, Virginia was flooded with wounded troops. Rampant inflation and severe food shortages caused crime to soar and threatened thousands with starvation. On April 2, 1863, a mob of one thousand women looted stores and warehouses in what became known as the Richmond Bread Riot.

Despite determined resistance and serious losses, Confederate forces had been pushed out of most of Tennessee by late 1863, depicted in this illustration.

Confederate Forces Collapse in Tennessee

LOSING CHATTANOOGA, GENERAL BRAGG
LEFT THE SOUTH OPEN FOR ATTACK.

General Braxton Bragg took command of the Confederate Army of Tennessee in the late summer of 1862. Although Bragg was a longtime friend of President Jefferson Davis, he quarreled with his fellow officers, who despised him, and was known for his failure of will in combat. His troops often booed and hissed when he rode through the ranks. Confederate cavalry commander Nathan Bedford Forrest once even threatened to whip Bragg—or worse.

Bragg's record on the field was equally unimpressive. His 1862 invasion of Kentucky had ended in failure, and during a Tennessee campaign in early 1863, he had lost almost 12,000 troops at the Battle of Stones River while gaining nothing.

During the summer of 1863, while Grant was besieging Vicksburg, Bragg and his army had been driven across Tennessee into Chattanooga. They were to remain there to defend the key port, but things did not start off well. When Major General William S. Rosecrans and his 60,000 men of the Federal Army of the Cumberland advanced on the city in September, Bragg was unnerved. He abandoned Chattanooga without a fight and retreated into north Georgia.

Unexpected Turn of Events

Then, unexpectedly, Bragg rebounded. His army had been reinforced by two divisions of seasoned troops sent from the east by General Lee under General James Longstreet. So, when Rosecrans and his army pursued Bragg into Georgia, Bragg was ready. From September 18 through 20, Bragg and his men overwhelmed Rosencrans' troops at the Battle of Chickamauga. Rosecrans retreated back to Chattanooga, which Bragg then besieged for the next two months.

After months of siege, Northern troops, reinforced by General Grant, successfully drove General Bragg's forces out of Chattanooga. These victorious Union solders posed for a picture atop Chattanooga's Lookout Mountain, the site of recent combat.

Union forces shipped Confederate prisoners of war to Northern prison camps following battles. These Southern soldiers were waiting at a Chattanooga, Tennessee railway depot.

The effort did not bring gains for the Confederates, however. General Grant, now commanding all Federal troops in the Western Theater, arrived on October 23 with reinforcements and drove Bragg away from Chattanooga. He then routed Bragg's army in a series of hard-fought battles—Orchard Knob, Lookout Mountain, and Missionary Ridge. The loss of Chattanooga and its important rail center was another major strategic blow to the Southerners. By late November, Bragg's beaten and depleted army retreated back into Georgia, and the Deep South stood open to Federal invasion.

Under General Braxton Bragg, Confederate forces lost the important rail center of Chattanooga. Bragg, opined a fellow officer, "was simply muddle-headed."

GENERAL NATHAN BEDFORD FORREST

1821-1877

Few officers on either side in the war matched the rise in rank achieved by Southern cavalry commander Nathan Bedford Forrest. Just shy of age 40 when he volunteered for Confederate service, Forrest soared from private to brigadier general in just over a year, and his extraordinary cavalry combat earned him the title Wizard of the Saddle.

7 THE HOME FRONT

THE WAGES OF WAR WERE NOT RESTRICTED TO CAMP AND BATTLEFIELD. CIVILIAN LIFE IN BOTH THE NORTH AND THE SOUTH WAS DRAMATICALLY ALTERED.

Southerners experienced hardships such as food shortages from the outset of the war. The Confederacy also suffered wild inflation and soaring cost of goods.

"O, if this war was over you and all the soldiers could come home. . . ."

—A lonely wife writing to her soldier husband, 1863

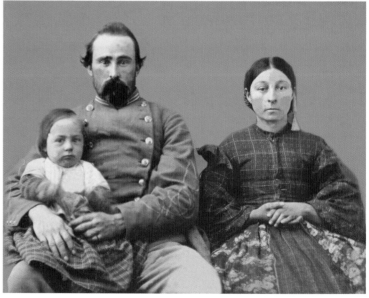

TOP: A Northern washerwoman attached to the Army of the Potomac worked alongside her three children. As civilian employees of the U.S. Army, laundresses received food, fuel, housing, and medical services. BOTTOM LEFT: Occasionally, wives and children were allowed to visit troops in camp. BOTTOM RIGHT: A Confederate officer posed for a family photograph with his wife and daughter.

SWORN INTO SERVICE

FOUR MILLION AMERICAN MEN
SAID GOOD-BYE TO THOSE AT HOME

From 1861 to 1865, it was common news in American families, North and South: A loved one was going to fight. In the war's opening days, many men eagerly rushed into military service. As the deadly reality of combat emerged in camp and on the battlefield, a sense of duty replaced the early enthusiasm for many; others went to fight because they were drafted. By war's end, almost 3,000,000 men served in the Northern armies, and approximately 1,000,000 fought for the South. More than 620,000 never returned home, and an estimated 500,000 came back wounded. The war reached into practically every home in America, and its impact often began with a letter such as this one, written by a Northern volunteer to his family.

New York, Sept. 1st, 1862

Dear Mother and Sisters:

I can no longer delay the task of communicating to you news which I fear you may regard as painful—a consideration which has hitherto deterred me from giving it. . . . I have accordingly entered the ranks—not rashly nor with the spirit of adventure, but with a cool head and under a strong sense of duty. No action of my life has been so well considered and deliberately taken.

My decision is, of course, irrevocable. I was sworn into the service of the United States on Saturday last as a private in the 9th Regiment, N.Y. Volunteers, now located at Fredericksburg, Va., in the Corps of General Burnside. The regiment was selected, 1st because it will take me at once where I can be useful; 2nd because its reputation for courage, based on actual test, assures me against being disgraced; 3rd because the class of men comprising it is much better than the average. . . .

It is not only desirable that our family should have a representative in the army, but where we are so well able to furnish one, it would be beyond endurance disgraceful . . . for young men living peacefully and selfishly at home, while the land is rent by fraction and threatened with ruin by violence. . . .

My course is marked out, and nothing mortal can alter it. Whatever may be your reflections do not conceive the idea that I am acting in haste to repent in leisure. I am both too old and have too much to sacrifice to take such a step merely from love of change.

In haste,
Ed K.W.

TOP: For those who could afford it, visiting the local photographer became a ritual as soldiers left for war. Here, a Northern private stood next to a young girl. MIDDLE: A Confederate officer posed with a Southern belle. BOTTOM: A Northern girl leaned lovingly against her father, a Federal musician and soldier.

A New York City street bustled with carriages, streetcars, wagons, and foot traffic.

The War Sparks a Booming Northern Economy

TO COVER THE TWO AND A HALF MILLION DOLLARS A DAY IT COST TO WAGE WAR, THE GOVERNMENT INTRODUCED TARIFFS AND PRINTED MONEY.

The North was stricken by a brief economic downturn in the war's opening days, but soon rebounded with a prolonged financial boom. Never, proclaimed the *New York Herald* in 1864, had New York City been "so crowded, so prosperous." The competing *New York Times* agreed: in the midst of "the most gigantic civil war the world has yet seen," the Northern people were living and eating well and had plenty to wear.

No longer hampered by its Southern members, who had resigned to join the Confederacy, the U.S. Congress promptly increased import tariffs to help cover the cost of war. Northern legislators also enacted America's first national income tax, and levied a revenue tax on virtually every item used in manufacturing and retailing—wood, leather, metal, textiles, iron, steel, stone, and more. A

license tax was required for every imaginable profession, from attorneys and bankers to horse traders and pawn brokers. Butchers paid a 10 cent tax for every hog sold, 5 cents for every sheep, and 30 cents for every cow. Even street jugglers had to pay the government a license fee to perform on the sidewalk.

The Federal government also printed massive amounts of paper money, borrowed huge sums at high interest, and sold war bonds. Flush with revenues, officials purchased uniforms, boots, rifles, revolvers, livestock, medicine, and countless other items in vast quantities.

The immense demand for products spurred the Industrial Revolution in America, giving rise to the assembly line and regional industries ranging from iron ore to railroad to flour milling. So much Northern corn

TOP: Northern civilians studied posted casualty lists outside a New York City newspaper office. BOTTOM: The work floor of the Starr Arms Company, a Northern firearms manufacturer in Yonkers, New York. The agricultural South could not begin to match the North's industrial output.

and wheat were grown during the war that the exported excess amounted to 40 percent of Great Britain's grain consumption.

"You are rushing into war with one of the most powerful, ingeniously mechanical and determined people on earth," a Northerner had warned a Southern acquaintance in 1860. "You are bound to fail." It was a prediction that proved correct.

MARY ANNE TODD
1818–1882

Mary Anne Todd, a well-educated Kentucky belle raised in a slave-owning family, married Abraham Lincoln in 1842.

As First Lady, Mary won praise as a charming society hostess who tastefully redecorated the executive mansion.

However, her time in and out of the White House was also marred by controversy and tragedy. Mary was criticized for both her lavish personal spending and her sometimes eccentric behavior. She had four sons with the president, but only one outlived her.

Ten years after Lincoln was assassinated, Mary was found to be insane and was briefly institutionalized, though her actual mental condition is still debated by historians and clinicians.

A new Capitol dome rose over wartime Washington, D.C. circa 1862.

Heartbreak and Sagging Morale in a Land of Plenty

FLUSH WITH CASH, CITY DWELLERS LIVED THE HIGH LIFE, PACKING CAFES AND BURLESQUE SHOWS.
THE LAVISH SPENDING MAY HAVE BEEN AN ATTEMPT TO ESCAPE THE HEARTBREAK OF WAR.

In the North's large cities, the wartime economic boom left many civilians momentarily flushed with cash. City dwellers packed saloons, playhouses, billiard parlors, minstrel theaters, and burlesque shows. In Washington, D.C., elegant dinners, balls, and soirees became the rage, and the flood of men in uniform expanded the capital's brothel trade. In New York City, crowds lined up to attend P.T. Barnum's Grand Colossal Museum and Menagerie, and swarmed Central Park for free band concerts.

"We have pushed our way downtown, dropping in at all the places of amusement," wrote a New York newspaper reporter, "and seeing them all jammed."

The economy was also boosted by tawdry wartime profiteering. Cotton confiscated from Southern planters could be bought in occupied areas for 20 cents a pound and sold in the North for a 500 percent markup. Unscrupulous manufacturers paid huge commissions to business brokers for wrangling government contracts. Crooked suppliers sold such poor-quality uniforms to the U.S. Army at the beginning of the war that the soldiers dubbed them "shoddies," and groused that they were fighting a rich-man's war.

"Every foul bird comes abroad, and every dirty reptile rises up," Abraham Lincoln aptly observed about wartime profiteering.

The lavish spending may have reflected more than just flush times: For many, it was likely an attempt to escape the heartbreak of war. No amount of profit could insulate Northern families from the loss of more than 300,000 young men, struck down by shot, shell, and disease, a staggering loss of life that befell almost every Northern home.

Likewise, even as Northern forces won victory after victory in the Western Theater, the defeats and disappointments in the Eastern Theater—and the shocking loss of life in general—progressively deflated enthusiasm for the war. Not until late 1864, when Federal forces captured the Deep South rail center of Atlanta, did Northern morale rebound.

P.T. Barnum's American Museum, shown in this artwork, was a wildly popular attraction in wartime New York City. It marked the first time African-American customers were admitted to the museum.

In the urban North, city-dwellers flocked to local parks for band concerts, patriotic rallies, and other forms of wartime recreation, as seen in this image from New York's Central Park.

In Northern cities such as Chicago, Cincinnati, Boston and New York, volunteers from the U.S. Sanitary Commission staged Metropolitan Fairs to raise funds for sick and wounded Northern soldiers.

With goods scarce, Southerners learned to improvise, making draperies into dresses and uniforms, resoling shoes with wood instead of leather, and producing candles from beeswax.

The Confederate Economy Crashes Quickly

SOUTHERNERS ENDURED THE IMPACT OF RUNAWAY INFLATION.

Financial conditions in the South, a Confederate official would bluntly recall, "went down steadily, rapidly, fatally" and never rebounded.

Confederate leaders had assumed that cotton sales to Britain would float the Southern economy, but English textile mills had amassed large emergency stores of cotton before the war, and "King Cotton" was dethroned by crops needed to feed Southern soldiers. Hampered by invasion and slowly strangled by the Federal naval blockade, the Southern economy came to a standstill.

Like their Northern counterparts, Southern leaders tried to finance the war with government bonds, taxation, short-term loans, and massive amounts of paper money, but nothing worked. The inherent

Southern suspicion of central government had placed restrictions on taxation in the Confederate States Constitution.

Borrowing money from state governments did little, government bonds lost their value, and excessive printing of Confederate currency only fueled debilitating inflation. In March of 1861, the Confederate States Congress authorized the printing of one million dollars in Confederate currency; five months later it ordered one hundred million more.

Desperate, the Richmond government churned out more and more currency until—in the words of a Confederate official—it was "spinning out the notes like a whirlwind in autumn."

QUEEN OF THE CONFEDERACY

Lucy Holcombe Pickens

1832–1899

Lucy Holcombe Pickens, one of the Confederacy's most celebrated women, was born in Tennessee and raised on a cotton plantation in eastern Texas. She completed her education at a finishing school in the North, and at age 25, married U.S. congressman Francis W. Pickens, who was a widower 27 years her senior. When Pickens was appointed U.S. ambassador to Russia, his new wife accompanied him to Saint Petersburg, becoming a favorite in the court of Czar Alexander II. In 1860, Ambassador Pickens returned to South Carolina, and was elected governor in time to preside over the Fort Sumter crisis.

As South Carolina's First Lady, Lucy Pickens was widely admired. She reportedly financed a regiment of troops—the Lucy Holcombe Legion—by selling jewelry given to her by the Russian Czar. In 1862, Confederate States Treasury Secretary Christopher Memminger honored her by adorning Confederate one-hundred and one-dollar treasury notes with her likeness, which led to her becoming known as the Queen of the Confederacy. A more lasting achievement, would be less well-known: She would be credited for introducing iced tea to Southern society.

TOP: Confederate currency of various denominations. Bottom: A $500 Confederate Treasury bond. Interest-bearing coupons attached to the bond were designed to be clipped and redeemed after the Confederacy won the war.

"I JUST LIKE TO BE FREE"

Slaves were affected by the same shortages that befell many Southerners

"We bring in some 500 prisoners, a good many refugees and about ten miles of Negroes," reported Federal general William T. Sherman in 1863.

Everywhere that Federal forces conducted operations, escaped slaves, officially called contrabands, fell in behind the blue-uniformed troops. Where possible, sprawling contraband camps were established, and some former slaves were put to work performing chores for the troops. Others were recruited into the Northern military.

Most Southern slaves, however, remained at home for a variety of reasons: their owners refused to free them; they were repelled by the destruction of private property by Federal armies; they felt they were ill-treated by Northern troops; or they simply had no place to go.

The severe hardship and shortages that befell other Southerners during the war also affected slaves. "We didn't have nothing to eat except hardtack and middin' meat," recalled former slave Sarah Debro. "I thought it 'twuz mule meat."

Even slaves who were loyal to their owners celebrated when freedom came: "I saw the Yankee soldiers [come]," former slave Melvin Smith would recall. "I heard some folks say that they stole their vittles, but they never bothered ours 'cause they had plenty of their own. Master called us together and said, 'You is free and can go if you want to.' Ol' Master was good and kind . . . but I just like to be free."

The ornate interior of St. Andrew's Hall in Charleston, S.C., where the South Carolina Secession Convention met in 1860. The hall was destroyed in a fire on December 11, 1861, along with five churches and 600 private homes. A New York newspaper suggested that the fire was divine retribution.

Skyrocketing Prices in the South

Meanwhile, runaway inflation caused the cost of common commodities to skyrocket. By 1865, a yard of cloth cost $60 in Confederate currency. A pound of butter was $35. A pair of shoes cost $800. The price of a barrel of flour was $1,400. In Richmond, hotel guests doing business in the capital complained that innkeepers would not accept payment at night because prices might need to be higher in the morning. Some Southerners turned to profiteering or hoarding.

"We fell into the habit of paying whatever was asked," a Southerner would recall, "knowing that tomorrow we should have to pay more." Such conditions undermined the Southern war effort and placed a debilitating burden on the Southern people that was unknown in the North.

A regiment of Zouave troops, the Louisiana Tigers, assembled on the street in New Orleans in 1861. Zouave originally referred to an infantry of the French army, made up of North African recruits. During the Civil War the term was applied to certain volunteer regiments who assumed a similar dress and drill as the original Zouave.

Among the first cities to be conquered by Union troops was Beaufort, South Carolina; when the coastal town was captured in late 1861, Northern commanders seized local homes to be used as officers' quarters.

Abigail "Abby" Hopper, seated center, was a leader in providing medical care for Northern soldiers. Because of her abolitionist sentiments, her home was burned during the 1863 Draft Riots.

Women at War: Spies, Scouts, Soldiers, and Heroic Homemakers

WOMEN ON THE HOMEFRONT BORE THE BURDEN OF WAR.

With so many men away, women across the land found themselves with increased responsibilities and new challenges. They took charge of their families, ran farms, operated stores, and oversaw plantations. Thousands worked as nurses; thousands more volunteered in groups like the U.S. Sanitary Commission or in sewing societies where they made soldiers' uniforms. Women went to work in factories, in treasury department offices, and even to war disguised as men: Northerner Sarah Emma Edmonds served in the 2nd Michigan Infantry, and Malinda Blalock masqueraded as a man to serve alongside her husband in the 26th North Carolina Infantry.

Untold numbers of women had wartime careers as spies and scouts. Former slave Harriet Tubman, famed for leading hundreds to freedom on the Underground Railroad, also served as a Northern spy in South Carolina and Georgia. Likewise, Union supporter Pauline Cushman served as spy and scout in the war's Western Theater—sometimes in the uniform of a Confederate soldier—and relived her experience on the stage after the war for audiences in the North.

Few women espionage agents could surpass the successes of Rose O'Neal Greenhow, a well-connected Washington, D.C. socialite. Greenhow not only organized a spy network that significantly contributed to the Confederate victory at First Bull Run, she served five months in Washington's Old Capitol Prison for her role, along with her young daughter. After Greenhow was released, she returned to the South, but drowned returning from a mission to Great Britain in 1864, when the blockade runner carrying her ran aground on the North Carolina coast.

Southern-born stage actress Pauline Cushman was a Northern spy who narrowly escaped being hanged by Confederate authorities.

Posing as a man, Malinda Blalock went to war with her husband, serving in the 26th North Carolina Infantry. Later, both deserted.

Rose O'Neal Greenhow used her position as a Washington, D.C. socialite to gather military information for the Confederacy—until she was imprisoned with her daughter.

Maria Isabella "Belle" Boyd was a successful Southern spy and courier in Virginia's Shenandoah Valley.

LEFT AND RIGHT: With most of the male population off at war, the women of the North and South were left to face the demands of the homefront. After the Civil War, many women were happy to return to their prewar roles. However, the women's suffrage movement gained significant momentum and women's participation in the workforce increased in the decades that followed.

With short furloughs, soldiers often couldn't travel home to see their families. When they could afford the travel, women and children would visit the men. The Northern officers' wives and children, like those pictured here, would sometimes stay for extended periods.

Spurning Soft Living

In many ways, the war was harder on women in the South than in the North. Serious food shortages were common. Basic necessities became unattainable. Business was suspended or destroyed. Education was interrupted. Daily life became a grueling ordeal. In Mobile, Atlanta, Richmond, and elsewhere, food riots occurred. Invading Northern armies destroyed the civilian infrastructure in many regions.

When Southern men departed to fight, their wives were left to guarantee their family's survival. To do so, they learned to improvise. They made draperies into dresses and uniforms and dyed them with boiled acorns or homegrown indigo. They resoled shoes with wood instead of leather, and produced candles from beeswax and rosin. They scraped the earth under old houses for salt, and used lye, lime, and wood ashes to make soap. Rose Frye, a South Carolina homemaker, would later recall how she and other women in the South "spurned soft living":

> The great difficulty lay in the fact that we had always looked to the North for everything, from a hair-pin to a shoestring, and from a candle to a cradle. The South was agricultural and not inventive . . . but with the war came a stoppage of all commercial intercourse between the two sections. The merchants' counters were quickly depleted.
>
> I went through the war on four calico dresses. We borrowed of each other. We braided straw for hats, and twisted a gay ribbon around the crown. We stitched incessantly. What a precious thing a needle was in those days. We picked cotton, carded and twisted it, and spun the yarn and wove the fabric. . . .
>
> My mother knit on average three pairs of socks per week for the boys in the field, whenever the material could be obtained. We spurned soft living [and] bore bravely every reverse of fortune. . . . We proved the truth of the old adage . . . that woman's ingenuity will surmount all obstacles.

VARINA HOWELL DAVIS
1826–1906

Confederate First Lady Varina Howell Davis, the daughter of a slave-owning Mississippi merchant, was educated in the North and married the widower Jefferson Davis in 1843, before he became president of the Confederacy.

As First Lady, Davis provoked controversy by questioning the South's ability to win the war. Even so, Southerners admired her intelligence, wit, and spirited personality.

Regimental bands were a fixture of military life in both Northern and Southern armies. Their music accompanied troops on drill and parade, broke the boredom of long marches, and cheered weary warriors following the horrors of battle.

Music to Soothe the Savage Beast of War

IN BOTH THE NORTH AND THE SOUTH, SONGS WERE WRITTEN THAT CONVEYED THE EXPERIENCE OF WARTIME, AND MUSIC INSPIRED AND CONSOLED BOTH NATIONS.

In the mid-19th century, music was a mainstay in both Northern and Southern culture. Piano makers sold more than 20,000 pianos a year to a population of some 30,000,000, and the sheet-music business thrived. Music was commonplace in theaters, concert halls, and saloons.

The most popular setting by far, however, was the family parlor, where Americans experienced their grief and joy to the strum of a banjo and piano chords. Favorite composers such as the North's prolific George F. Root and Southerner Harry Macarthy accommodated the public mood with songs that reflected the events of the day.

Popular patriotic songs included "Battle Hymn of the Republic," "Bonnie Blue Flag," and "Dixie." Soldier life was tenderly treated in tunes such as "Just Before the Battle, Mother," "Lorena," "Tramp, Tramp, Tramp." A few works were political, such as "John Brown's Body," and "Maryland, My Maryland." The suffering and sacrifices of the home front were expressed in popular tunes such as "When This Cruel War is Over" and "Can I Go, Dearest Mother." Emancipation was celebrated in "Kingdom Coming" and "Sixty-Three is the Jubilee."

Nothing of course could fully ease the absence of a loved one. The most popular song on both sides was "Home, Sweet Home."

In the Confederacy, music lovers celebrated the quest for Southern nationhood with sheet music to this rousing tune by composer Harry Macarthy. "The Bonnie Blue Flag" refers to the unofficial Confederate banner in 1861.

"The Star-Spangled Banner" was not made the national anthem until 1889. This 1862 edition of the sheet music features a Union soldier on the cover.

On the eve of the Civil War, Americans bought more than 20,000 pianos a year. In homes throughout the North and the South, the war was celebrated, mourned, and endured with music.

JULIA WARD HOWE
1819-1910

In 1861, when New Yorker Julia Ward Howe visited Northern troops in Washington, D.C., she was already a published author. Howe was so inspired by the soldiers' service she retired to her room at Washington's Willard Hotel and wrote the poem that became the immensely popular "Battle Hymn of the Republic."

Refugees from the 1862 Dakota War in Minnesota rested under the protection of Northern troops. More than 500 Minnesota settlers and uncounted numbers of the Dakota tribe were killed in the uprising.

Indian Raids Terrorize Unprotected Civilians on the Frontier

WITH MEN AWAY AT WAR, FRONTIER FAMILIES WERE VULNERABLE.

Women and children living on America's frontier during the Civil War faced a unique threat when the men of the family left for service: deadly Indian raids.

Near-starvation conditions on Minnesota's Dakota reservation sparked an uprising in the summer of 1862, and Sioux raiders slaughtered numerous white farming families along the Minnesota River Valley. Thousands of civilians fled their homes and several hundred Dakota and Sioux were also killed.

In Confederate Texas, the absence of men and frontier troops encouraged the Comanche to increase their assaults on isolated farms and ranches. A survivor of a typical attack recalled:

"We children had heard screams and war whoops and were running as fast as we could to the nearest hiding place. . . . Ma heard the commotion, saw the Indians and came running back toward the house, screaming, 'My babies! My babies!' But she never reached the house. Three Indian arrows brought her down dead a few feet from the front door."

In an attempt to reduce Indian attacks on the frontier during the Civil War, the Lincoln administration entertained a delegation of Cheyenne and Kiowa leaders at the White House. This image, taken in the Executive Mansion conservatory, shows President Lincoln's private secretary, John George Nicolay, in the center rear.

Confederate soldiers Private Thomas F. Bates, left, of the 6th Texas Infantry and Private Simeon J. Crews, right, of the 7th Texas Cavalry posed with weapons.

LOUISA MAY ALCOTT

1832–1888

Northern author Louisa May Alcott, who would earn fame for her Civil War novel *Little Women*, temporarily served as a nurse for the sick and wounded at a Washington, D.C. soldiers' hospital. While there, Alcott contracted typhoid fever, which would cause her health problems throughout the remainder of her life.

ABOVE LEFT, ABOVE RIGHT: Chambersburg, Pennsylvania lay in ruins in 1864. It was the only Northern town destroyed during the war.

Confederate forces put the torch to the Pennsylvania town of Chambersburg after the town's residents failed to raise the sum of $100,000 in gold demanded by the invading Southerners.

War Invades Civilian Life

WHEN GENERAL WILLIAM SHERMAN'S ARMY FORCED THE EVACUATION
OF ATLANTA, CITY OFFICIALS PLED FOR MERCY. SHERMAN REFUSED.

At times the war led soldiers and commanders to commit acts they would normally have denounced. In May of 1864, under orders from General Grant, an 18,000-man Northern army swept through Virginia's Shenandoah Valley, setting fire to military targets while plundering and burning private homes.

The raid sparked a vicious cycle of retaliation. A week later, Confederate troops burned Chambersburg, Pennsylvania, destroying more than four hundred structures. Grant then sent an army of more than 40,000 troops to the Shenandoah with orders to "leave the Valley a barren waste." The troops did so, destroying virtually everything along a 90-mile-long line of march, including some 2,000 barns, private homes, and an estimated 3,000 sheep.

Removing the Citizens of Atlanta

One of the war's most controversial acts toward noncombatants followed the capture of Atlanta by General William T. Sherman's army in 1864. Sherman ordered a forced evacuation of the city's entire civilian population. City officials pled for mercy, but Sherman refused, stating: "War is cruelty and you cannot refine it."

People fled the city. "The scene around the depot for days previous to its final abandonment was heartrending in the extreme," reported a Northern newspaper correspondent. "Old age and tottering infancy huddled together, awaiting their chance of escape. They cast many a long and lingering look at their once-happy home, which they were now about to abandon, perhaps forever."

After General William T. Sherman captured Atlanta, he ordered the forced evacuation of the city's entire civilian population. Northern troops destroyed Atlanta's rail station and tore up the city's railroad tracks.

ATLANTA BURNING

The 1939 film *Gone With the Wind* captures the burning of the city of Atlanta at the hands of Sherman's troops. The first scene of the movie to be filmed, David O. Selznick simulated the terror of a city ablaze by setting fire to an RKO Pictures back lot, upon which the film's sets would later be built.

ABOVE: In 1863, following the Battle of Gettysburg, this photo was found clutched in the hand of a dead Northern soldier. Stories of the image sparked a search for the identities of the man and his children throughout the North. RIGHT: Northern civilians lined up outside a newspaper office to read the latest war news in this illustration.

THE FACES OF WAR

The Children of the Battlefield

A POIGNANT PHOTOGRAPH CAPTIVATED
THE NORTHERN HOME FRONT.

Midway through the war, the grief that flooded wartime America was personalized in the North by a single incident. As Federal burial details went about their grim chores after the Battle of Gettysburg, the body of a Northern soldier was found clutching an ambrotype of three small children. The soldier was unidentified, but he had been mortally wounded and seemed to have spent his dying moments gazing at a photograph of his children—two boys and a girl.

The image made its way to the *Philadelphia Inquirer,* which reported the sad story under the headline "Whose Father Was He?" The limited technology of the day prevented the newspaper from publishing the photograph, but the writer carefully described its details. Other newspapers picked up the story, and it became a sensation in the North, igniting a nationwide inquiry for the identity of the fallen father of the "Children of the Battlefield."

Finally, in November of 1863, the search ended: The soldier was Sergeant Amos Humiston of Portville, New York, who had fought at Gettysburg in the 154th New York Infantry. The three "Children of the Battlefied" were his eight-year-old Frank, four-year-old Frederick, and six-year-old Alice. Sergeant Humiston's widow, Philinda, had not heard from him since before the Battle of Gettysburg, and learned of his death only when a neighbor read about the photograph.

The event inspired popular sheet music entitled "The Children of the Battlefield," and proceeds from its sale were sent to the children and their widowed mother, who was given a job at an orphanage until she remarried.

8

1864: THE COLLAPSE OF THE CONFEDERACY

GRANT WAS PROMOTED TO GENERAL-IN-CHIEF OF ALL NORTHERN ARMIES AND WENT HEAD-TO-HEAD
WITH A WORTHY ADVERSARY, ROBERT E. LEE.

Sherman's troops marched through Georgia, evacuating towns as they went. While Union soldiers burned the city of Atlanta, the Hood's Ordnance train, shown here, was destroyed by evacuating rebel forces.

"I propose to fight it out on this line if it takes all summer."

—Federal lieutenant general Ulysses S. Grant, 1864

General Grant and his staff officers, seated on benches dragged from a Virginia church, discussed strategy. Grant, left of center, was stooped to study a military map.

A Leader With a Vision

WHEN ULYSSES S. GRANT WAS PROMOTED TO COMMANDER OF ALL UNION TROOPS, HE ACCEPTED ON THE CONDITION THAT HE WOULD WORK FROM THE FIELD, NOT FROM WASHINGTON.

By spring 1864, Major General Ulysses S. Grant had overseen a Northern victory in the Western Theater and President Lincoln wanted the winning streak to continue, in the East and everywhere else.

To facilitate Grant's success, Lincoln decided to hand him control of all Union troops. On March 10, he named Grant General-in-Chief of all Northern armies, a title that elevated him above other generals. The position, which had not been held since George Washington, had to be revived with congressional legislation.

Grant accepted the promotion on the condition that he must direct the war from the field, not from Washington; life in the capital did not suit his style.

His disdain for dress uniforms was well known to his staff: Instead, he usually wore a rumpled private's uniform, its pockets stuffed with cigars, with his general's stars affixed to his shoulders. Now he had three stars—the only man in the U.S. Army so ranked—and he would lead from where he pleased.

Grant promptly joined the Army of the Potomac in Virginia. He kept General Meade, the victor of Gettysburg, as the official head of the army, but took control of directing its operations.

Reaction to Grant's leadership in the ranks was mixed: Some generals thought he would do no better against Robert E. Lee than any of his predecessors. A Northern private, seeing Grant ride by for the first time, thought differently. Studying the bearded, determined-looking officer as he passed, the private noted simply, "He looks as if he means it."

General George Meade officially remained in command of the Army of the Potomac, but Grant—Meade's superior—held overall command in the field.

General Ulysses S. Grant kept his headquarters in the field during the war. Often at his side was General John Rawlins, pictured here along with a lieutenant at Grant's camp in Cold Harbor. Rawlins was Grant's personal aide and close friend, who reportedly also helped Grant abstain from drinking too much during battle.

1864

January

1864: A Test of Wills and Forces

Grant was outmaneuvered by Lee in Virginia, but he turned the tide with the capture of Atlanta and Savannah.

MARCH 10 Ulysses S. Grant promoted to rank of General-in-Chief of the U.S. Army to oversee operations on both fronts.

MAY 4–5 The first face-off between Grant and General Robert E. Lee, the Battle of the Wilderness, in Virginia, ended with bloody losses for both, but a victory for the South.

April

MAY 7 Grant ordered General William T. Sherman to take Atlanta and its critically important rail center.

MAY 8–19 Grant continued the Overland Campaign in Virginia at Spotsylvania Court House, but failed to outwit Lee in a costly but inconclusive battle.

JUNE 1–3 The Overland Campaign sputtered at the Battle of Cold Harbor, where the North lost 20,000 troops and the South 5,000.

JUNE 15 Fighting began at Petersburg, Virginia, where Confederate troops dug into trenches and outfought Union forces.

August

SEPTEMBER 1 Northern troops captured Atlanta in a major strategic and symbolic victory.

NOVEMBER 8 In a landslide, Abraham Lincoln reelected president.

NOVEMBER 16 Sherman launched his controversial March to the Sea, terrifying Southern citizens with slash-and-burn tactics.

NOVEMBER 30 Confederate forces suffered crippling blows to their ranks, losing six leaders in a day, at the Battle of Franklin in Tennessee.

DECEMBER 21 Sherman's March to the Sea ended in the capture of Savannah, Georgia, another strategic victory for the North.

December

Grant Versus Lee: The First Battle

THE VICTOR OF THE WEST ENCOUNTERED THE MILITARY GENIUS OF THE EAST.

I n the spring of 1864, General-in-Chief Ulysses S. Grant ordered a Federal advance on all fronts. He put the Western Theater under the command of General William T. Sherman, instructing him to drive the Confederate Army of Tennessee out of north Georgia and to advance on the vitally important Confederate rail center of Atlanta. Grant himself turned his attentions to Virginia in an initiative that would become known as the Overland Campaign. There, he set out to destroy General Robert E. Lee's Army of Northern Virginia and to capture the Confederate capital of Richmond.

On May 4, Grant put the Army of the Potomac on the march, heading southward with 118,000 well-armed, well-equipped troops—roughly double Lee's 60,000-man army. Lee, however, learned of the Union army movements, and readied his soldiers for the fight.

The most accomplished general of the Union army was about to square off against the most successful general of the Confederacy.

TOP LEFT: Grant was the only three-star general in the U.S. Army. BOTTOM LEFT: Confederate general Robert E. Lee led the Army of Northern Virginia, with 60,000 troops compared to Grant's 118,000. ABOVE: The Army of the Potomac was heralded as "the finest army on the planet" but had suffered from poor leadership.

MAJOR GENERAL FRANZ SIGEL

1824–1902

On May 15, 1864, Northern troops under Major General Franz Sigel were turned back at the Battle of New Market in Virginia's Shenandoah Valley—thanks in no small way to cadets from the Virginia Military Institute. Ordered into the fighting as reinforcements, the cadets captured a Federal artillery battery and helped drive Sigel's Federals from the valley. Nine men were killed and another 48 wounded, but their heroism would inspire future VMI cadets.

TOP LEFT: General William T. Sherman, selected by Grant to take charge of Federal armies in the Western Theater, was ordered to advance on the Confederate rail center of Atlanta. TOP RIGHT: General Joseph E. Johnston and the Confederate Army of Tennessee stubbornly opposed Sherman's advance through north Georgia. BOTTOM: To block the Federal advance on Atlanta, General Johnston's Confederates erected defensive earthworks, but they did not stop Sherman's army.

No Turning Back

Grant planned to move his troops quickly around the Confederate flank and advance on Richmond but was caught by surprise when Lee shifted his forces to meet the operation head-on.

On May 5, 1864, the two armies collided northwest of Fredericksburg at the Battle of the Wilderness, named for the dense undergrowth of the region. The ensuing combat was fierce, and both sides suffered heavy casualties. Hundreds of soldiers burned to death during battle when the underbrush caught fire, set ablaze by artillery. "The usually silent Wilderness," recalled a Confederate officer, "had suddenly become alive with the angry flashing and heavy roar of the musketry, mingled with the yells of the combatants as they swayed to and fro in the gloomy thickets."

When Lee's army refused to back down after two unbroken days of fighting, Grant was forced to withdraw his men. He had lost 18,000 troops to Lee's 7,000. Many Northern soldiers thought the battle a defeat—what one soldier called "another skedaddle"—and expected to retreat northward, as they had in the past. But they did not know their new commander: Grant was willing to inflict and incur losses on a scale unseen in the preceding two years. He would leverage his superior numbers.

Instead of retreating, Grant ordered the army to march southeast, in the hopes of turning Lee's flank and battling again. Back in Washington, Lincoln was disappointed by Grant's failure—but he was heartened to receive a report from Grant that stood in contrast with those of his predecessors: "Whatever happens," Grant notified Lincoln, "there will be no turning back."

LEFT: On May 4, 1864, General Grant led the Army of the Potomac across Virginia's Rapidan River, launching his Overland Campaign against Richmond and General Robert E. Lee's army. RIGHT: The first confrontation between Grant and Lee occurred at the Battle of the Wilderness, fought northwest of Fredericksburg, in a region notorious for its dense thickets.

BELOW: Underbrush caught fire during the Battle of the Wilderness and wounded soldiers on both sides were burned alive. Combat artist Alfred R. Waud created this eyewitness illustration of Northern troops rescuing their comrades from the killer blaze.

The Battle of Spotsylvania Court House

AFTER FREDERICKSBURG, LEE RUSHED HIS MEN TO A RURAL CROSSROADS COMMUNITY,
BUILT A STRONG LINE, AND ONCE AGAIN TRIUMPHED OVER GRANT.

L ee did not simply wait on Grant's next move. Using his cavalry to slow the Federal advance, the Confederate strategist put his army on a rapid march from the Wilderness to a rural crossroads community named Spotsylvania Court House. His troops quickly built formidable earthworks along a long defensive line, and readied to meet the Northern army head-on.

The Bloody Angle

Beginning on the night of May 8, Grant pounded the Southerners in a series of brutal assaults. At a section of Lee's line known as the Mule Shoe Salient, the fire was so ferocious that soldiers were "chopped into hash by the bullets," a survivor would recall. So many bullets whittled away at a nearby oak tree that it toppled over.

At a position that would become infamous as "Bloody Angle," the dead of both sides were stacked like cordwood. Below piles of corpses, "the convulsive twitching of limbs and the writhing of bodies [revealed] wounded men struggling to extricate themselves," reported a horrified survivor.

Again, the Northern troops were unable to overcome their Confederate foes and when the Battle of Spotsylvania finally ended on May 19, Grant's army had failed to break Lee's line or defeat his army. He lost another 18,000 troops, compared to Lee's 12,000. But Grant still would not give up. After a few days of rest, he redeployed his men—racing once more to flank Lee's army and do battle. "I propose to fight it out on this line all summer," he notified Lincoln.

LEFT: The Battle of Spotsylvania Court House in Virginia was the second major strike in General Grant's Overland Campaign.
RIGHT: Union soldiers from the 1st Massachusetts Artillery bury the dead following the final Federal attack on May 18.

These Southern soldiers were among the 20,000 troops
killed at the Battle of Spotsylvania Court House.

TOP: Some of the bloodiest hand-to-hand combat of the Civil War occurred at the Battle of Spotsylvania at a sector of Lee's line known as the Mule Shoe Salient. Amid a pounding rainstorm, Northern and Southern soldiers sometimes trampled their own wounded beneath the mud, captured in this painting. BOTTOM LEFT: An unexploded artillery shell was left embedded in a tree. BOTTOM RIGHT: A dead Southern soldier with his Enfield rifle at his feet.

Northern grave-diggers buried the dead following the prolonged fighting at Spotsylvania Court House.

WITNESS TO WAR

In the "Mule Shoe" at Spotsylvania

A CONFEDERATE SOLDIER RECOUNTED THE BRAVERY AND SUFFERING OF THE FOES HE FACED AT ONE OF THE WAR'S MORE GRUESOME BATTLES.

Nowhere was the horror of Civil War combat more evident than at the Battle of Spotsylvania. Private David E. Holt of the 16th Mississippi Infantry, a survivor of the fighting in the Mule Shoe Salient, later recorded a grim account excerpted here:

In one of the persistent charges of the enemy, the United States flag was held by a brave soldier on one side of our flag, and the state flag of New York was held by another gallant Yankee on the other side, the three waving together, but not for long. The men that held them were shot down, and the two flags of the enemy fell in the mud. Our flag bearer was shot down again and another man grabbed the flag and swung it aloft. . . .

We could hear the screams of the wounded over all that infernal noise. They were trampled by their oncoming comrades. Often the dead lay on the wounded. When there would be any kind of a lull in the fighting, as when the Yanks reformed their line, there floated over to use the faint, pitiful cries of the wounded, and often a painful please of "Oh, for God's sake, take this dead man off of me!" . . .

It was still drizzling rain and a thin mist [hung] over everything. There lay the tree cut down by bullets and the bloody ditch and the many dead and wounded. One wounded man was cursing, another praying to the Blessed Virgin. Many were crying for water, some begging to have the dead taken off them. I don't expect to go to hell, but if I do, I am sure that Hell can't beat that terrible scene. . . .

CALVARY CLASH AT YELLOW TAVERN

While Northern and Southern troops were engaged in the Battle of Spotsylvania Court House in May of 1864, Federal cavalry under Major General Philip Sheridan embarked on a raid against Richmond's defenses. The operation was of little importance— except for a cavalry clash at nearby Yellow Tavern. There, on May 11, 1864, the famed Southern cavalry commander, Major General J.E.B. Stuart was mortally wounded.

TOP: To prepare for an infantry assault at Cold Harbor, Federal artillery bombarded the Confederate line, as seen in this artwork. General Grant ordered one attack after another; in the words of an eyewitness, Northern soldiers "went down like rows of blocks." BOTTOM: Northern burial details unearthed earlier graves even as they attempted to bury those recently killed.

The Butchery of Cold Harbor

BEFORE HEADING INTO THIS GRIM BATTLE, UNION SOLDIERS WROTE THEIR NAMES ON SLIPS OF PAPER SO THEY COULD BE IDENTIFIED FOR NEXT-OF-KIN.

The third face-off between Grant and Lee took place at Cold Harbor, Virginia, and ended much as the first two did: with a Confederate victory.

Grant planned to flank and overcome Lee's army with an unprecedented show of force. In one assault, he unleashed more than 40,000 soldiers who advanced shoulder-to-shoulder in a six-mile-long line. Before making the charge, many of the Northern troops wrote their names on slips of paper and pinned them on their uniforms, certain they would be killed and hoping their name tags would identify them for next-of-kin.

But the effort was doomed. By the time Grant got his men into place, Confederate troops had already erected near-impregnable fortifications and they turned back Grant's repeated frontal attacks. In a last attempt to turn the tide, Grant ordered another charge—one that took the lives of 7,000 men in eight minutes. "It could not be called a battle," a Northern survivor recounted later. "It was simply butchery. . . ."

In the trio of defeats of the Overland Campaign, Grant had lost a shocking 50,000 troops to Lee's 32,000. But he had also gained an edge. With his seemingly endless reserves, Grant could replace his men, while Lee could not. Grant refused to retreat. "We have met a man, this time," noted one of Lee's officers, "who either does not know when he is whipped, or cares not if he loses his whole army."

During the Overland Campaign, Grant transferred heavy artillery regiments from Washington, D.C. to reinforce the Army of the Potomac. At the Battle of Cold Harbor, they were used as infantry in frontal assaults against Lee's entrenched troops.

An illustration of the fighting at Cold Harbor, when 7th New York Heavy Artillery temporarily captured a portion of the Confederate line. "We felt it was murder, not war . . . ," recounted a New Yorker.

Grant's Overland Campaign failed to defeat Lee's army or capture Richmond, but it severely depleted Lee's manpower. Confederate troops were forced to hunker down in a series of trenches.

Stalemate at Petersburg

GRANT THOUGHT HE COULD CAPTURE RICHMOND BY TAKING A NEARBY TRANSPORTATION HUB, BUT THE OFFENSIVE BOGGED DOWN IN TRENCH WARFARE.

In mid-June of 1864, General Grant began to reconsider his strategy. He had thrown his army against Lee's defensive lines for more than a month and all he had to show for it was a stunning casualty toll. Worse, he had been unable to capture the strategically important city of Richmond.

Finally, he concluded that the key to seizing the Confederate capital was Petersburg, located twenty miles to the south. The city was home to a rail link that transported Lee's army and most of the supplies that were shipped from the south to the soldiers in Richmond. Grant believed that if he could capture Petersburg, he could simultaneously advance on Richmond from the south while reducing Lee's army with constant fighting.

On June 15, he launched an attack on what he thought would be a weak portion of Lee's defensive line at Petersburg. The assault fumbled and failed, and by June 18, Lee had moved his headquarters from Richmond to Petersburg. The confrontation developed into a bloody, ten-month siege. In spite of thinning reinforcements, Lee was able to engineer a formidable defensive line of trenches and earthworks and his men repelled Grant's onslaughts. Southern resistance was crumbling elsewhere, but in Virginia, to the dismay of the Northern public, Grant, was unable to immediately defeat Robert E. Lee.

By late 1864, Lee and his Army of Northern Virginia were burrowed into a vast network of defenses at Petersburg and were resisting Grant's attempts to capture Richmond.

During the ten-month siege, soldiers lived and fought in the trenches and earthworks outside Petersburg.

The grizzly realities of trench warfare took their toll on Union and Confederate troops who clashed at Petersburg.

THE BATTLE OF THE CRATER

A Spectacular Explosion Becomes a Spectacular Northern Defeat

Early in the assault on Petersburg, Grant was frustrated by his failure to break Lee's line and agreed to an odd but daring maneuver to reverse the tide. He deployed a regiment of former Pennsylvania coal miners to dig a 500-foot tunnel beneath the no-man's land separating the two armies. Under the supervision of a lieutenant colonel who had been a mining engineer before the war, Northern troops excavated a cavern below a key section of the Confederate line. They then packed it with 320 barrels of gunpowder. Grant hoped the giant bomb would blow a huge opening in the Confederate defenses, enabling Northern troops to swarm through the hole left by the blast, overwhelm Lee's army, and capture Petersburg and Richmond.

At 4:44 AM on July 30, 1864, the so-called Petersburg Mine was detonated. It was a fearsome explosion. Smoke, dirt, debris, bodies, and body parts gushed upward in a gigantic upheaval that created a canyon-like crater, opened a wide break in Lee's defensive line, and stunned the surviving defenders.

Unfortunately for Grant, the Federal troops rushed into the hollow, but were unable to scale the walls on the opposite side and found themselves trapped. When the Southerners recovered, they were able to fire at the Union soldiers from atop the crater's rim. The Battle of the Crater, as it became known, proved to be a Northern disaster. Lee lost less than 1,500 troops, while Grant's army suffered almost 4,000 casualties and accomplished nothing.

Northern troops poured into the Crater at Petersburg, after exploding a giant underground bomb, shown here in this illustration. The surprise attack, however, ended in a Northern defeat.

General William T. Sherman and his staff officers surveyed the battlefield outside Atlanta in the fall of 1864. After months of maneuvering and savage fighting, Sherman's army finally captured the Deep South's premier rail and munitions center.

The Capture of Atlanta

IN AN ATTEMPT TO SAVE THE CRITICAL RAIL CENTER, CONFEDERATE PRESIDENT JEFFERSON DAVIS BROUGHT IN A NEW GENERAL.

As General Grant battled Lee's army in Virginia during the spring of 1864, Major General William T. Sherman and his army were in north Georgia. Their orders from Grant were to capture Atlanta and its critically important rail center, and to "get into the interior of the enemy's country as far as you can, inflicting all the damage you can. . . ."

Sherman commanded three armies—the Army of the Tennessee, the Army of the Cumberland, and the Army of the Ohio—comprising more than 100,000 troops. The opposing Confederate Army of Tennessee, led by General Joseph E. Johnston, numbered about half that. Even so, Johnston, an experienced commander who had taken over from General Braxton Bragg, managed to batter and delay Sherman's forces as they advanced through the mountainous terrain.

The show was not enough for Confederate president Jefferson Davis, who was fearful of losing Atlanta. He removed Johnston and replaced him with General John Bell Hood, a solemn, one-legged commander who rode into combat tied to his saddle.

After a series of bloody battles, Hood abandoned Atlanta on September 1, 1864. Three weeks later, he led his army northward into Tennessee, hoping to lure Union forces into following them out of the city. Sherman did not take the bait: He pursued Hood only briefly, then left him and his army to face Northern forces already in Tennessee.

Confederate general John Bell Hood was President Davis's choice to replace Joseph Johnston, who kept Sherman at bay, but failed to save Atlanta.

General Hood's army headquarters in Atlanta were seized by Union troops and hung with the U.S. flag.

A 12-pounder field artillery piece pointed over abandoned Confederate earthworks outside Atlanta. In September of 1864, Hood's Confederates were forced to give up Atlanta, opening the Deep South to Federal invasion.

GENERAL JOHN BELL HOOD

1831–1879

A Kentucky native, John Bell Hood graduated West Point at 22. He served in the U.S. military until spring of 1861, when he resigned his post to become cavalry captain in the Confederacy.

He became one of the most quickly promoted military men of the Civil War, though his effectiveness seemed to decrease as he rose in position. Wounded in battle at Gettysburg and then Chickamauga, he later headed up offensives intended to halt General William T. Sherman's advances on Atlanta, all of which failed with heavy casualties.

Hood surrendered to Northern forces in the spring of 1865 and lived out the rest of his days in New Orleans with his family.

A major Southern transportation hub, the Atlanta railroad was destroyed by Sherman's troops. The fire spread throughout the city.

Atlanta in Ruins

From Atlanta, Sherman triumphantly telegraphed Washington: "Atlanta is ours and fairly won." It was a severe blow to the Confederacy, shutting down the young nation's central transportation hub and symbolically crushing a Southern stronghold. The Northern victory also bolstered public support for the war, which had begun to flag with endless fighting.

Sherman ordered a forced evacuation of the city, sending refugees away in droves by road and rail. On November 15, his troops set fire to Atlanta's railroad facilities, industrial sites, and business district. The flames spread through the city, leaving it—in the words of one resident—nothing but a "dirty, dusty ruin."

With "the heart of the Southern States," as a *New York Times* reporter had called Atlanta, smoldering behind them, Sherman and his 60,000-man army marched out, en route to Savannah.

Atlanta residents piled their luggage atop the last train from the city before fleeing for safety.

In the wake of Atlanta's capture by Sherman's army, the city streets were empty except for Federal supply wagons. In November of 1864, General Sherman ordered Atlanta's civilian population forcibly evacuated—then much of the city was burned.

Before Sherman's men set off on their controversial March to the Sea, they torched Atlanta's sprawling railway station.

HORACE GREELY

1811-1872

In July of 1864, Horace Greeley, the influential editor of the *New York Tribune,* traveled to the Canadian side of Niagara Falls to meet with agents of the Confederate government. Greeley hoped that he could use his position as a newspaper editor to broker a peace treaty between the North and the South, but his attempts at peace negotiations achieved nothing.

LEFT, MIDDLE: 1864 campaign posters for General George B. McClellan and the Democrats, left, and Abraham Lincoln and the Republicans, right. TOP RIGHT: 1864 campaign button for Abraham Lincoln BOTTOM RIGHT: Democratic challenger McClellan

Both candidates on the 1864 vice presidential ticket, George Pendleton, left, and Andrew Johnson, right, were Democrats.

The Surprising Presidential Election of 1864

THE YOUNG NAPOLEON CHALLENGED "THE GREAT BABOON" IN WHAT WOULD BE AN ELECTORAL COLLEGE LANDSLIDE.

As the 1864 presidential contest approached, Abraham Lincoln feared he would not win reelection. Considered an exceptional leader and a superb commander in chief by some of the electorate, Lincoln had almost single-handedly kept the Northern war effort alive when newspaper editors, the general public, and even his own cabinet members had despaired of victory.

Others, however, viewed the former Illinois lawyer as a hayseed from the prairie unfit for the office. His move to imprison an estimated 20,000 Northerners without trial on disloyalty charges was controversial. His support for a military draft had ignited riots in Northern cities, and his Emancipation Proclamation had spurred droves of Northern soldiers to desert.

After General Grant's highly anticipated 1864 spring offensive failed to end the war, Northern discontent again increased. One opposition newspaper even reviled Lincoln as "the Great Baboon."

A Well Known Opponent

Lincoln's opponent in the 1864 presidential election was the popular Northern general George B. McClellan, whom Lincoln had dismissed for his military failures. Celebrated as "the Young Napoleon," McClellan, 41, was bright, charismatic, and politically well-connected. He had the support of mainstream Democrats and the party's peace faction, which wanted to negotiate a ceasefire with the Confederacy. In the summer of 1864, it looked like McClellan and the Democrats were poised to take the presidency.

Then, with the capture of Atlanta in September, public opinion began to shift. Increasing numbers of Northerners thought the war was winnable. Lincoln also made it convenient for Union soldiers to vote, a popular move which created potential new support. When the electoral college numbers were tallied, General McClellan carried only three states. Lincoln won with 212 votes to McClellan's 12. It was a landslide: Lincoln would continue to lead the North and the war.

General George B. McClellan, here with his wife Nelly, was a popular Democrat and won 45 percent of the popular vote against Lincoln, but he lost in the electoral college.

An illustration showed Northern troops lining up to vote in the 1864 presidential election. Soldiers voted heavily for Lincoln.

General John Bell Hood's Confederate Army of Tennessee suffered devastating casualties at the Battle of Franklin shown above in this painting by Howard Pyle.

The Battles of Franklin and Nashville

A SOUTHERN ARMY DASHED
ITSELF TO PIECES.

After the presidential election, Southern general John Bell Hood hoped to lure Sherman and his army away from Atlanta by taking the Confederate Army of Tennessee through north Georgia and back into Tennessee. There, he found ample Federal troops ready to fight, and on November 30, 1864, launched the Battle of Franklin, a massive assault on the Federal Army of the Ohio.

Hood, who had no supporting artillery, ordered 18,000 troops to make a frontal assault over two miles of open fields. But the Northern breastworks proved impregnable and Hood's army was shredded: He not only lost 32 Confederate battle flags, he suffered 6,200 casualties compared to 2,300 for the North, and sacrificed the lives of six Confederate generals, including Major General Patrick Cleburne, known as the "Stonewall of the West."

Hood moved on, trying to take his army northward, but he could not bypass the Northern forces concentrated at Nashville. On December 15 and 16, Hood's army was attacked by the Federal Army of the Cumberland. The Confederate Army of Tennessee was almost annihilated, losing another 6,000 troops. Hood and the survivors retreated southward.

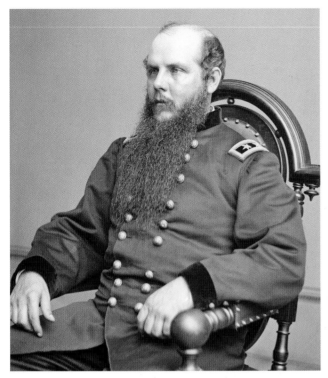

The Battle of Franklin was a disaster for General John Bell Hood, who deployed 18,000 Southern troops to attack the Army of the Ohio under Major General John Schofield, above. The two-mile-long assault cost Hood more than 6,000 troops and six generals.

The Tennessee state capitol rose above Nashville, which had been occupied by Northern armies for nearly two years in 1864. The city was photographed by George Barnard, who was traveling with Sherman's Army of the Cumberland.

CIVIL WAR STATS:

SIX SOUTHERN GENERALS KILLED IN A SINGLE BATTLE

Six Confederate generals were killed at the Battle of Franklin—more than in any other engagement of the Civil War. Six more were wounded, and another was captured. The six who were killed:

MAJOR GENERAL PATRICK CLEBURNE

1828–1864
An Irish immigrant who joined the Confederate cause, Cleburne was known for his battlefield strategy. His nickname was the "Stonewall of the West."

BRIGADIER GENERAL JOHN ADAMS

1825–1864
Rewarded for gallantry in the Mexican-American War in the U.S. Army, he joined Confederate forces in early 1861. His brigade led the march into Tennessee.

BRIGADIER GENERAL STATES RIGHTS GIST

1831–1864
Named for his family's politics, Gist was a lawyer in South Carolina. He was also a militia general before the war.

BRIGADIER GENERAL HIRAM GRANBURY

1831–1864
Born in Mississippi, Granbury moved to Texas, where, when the state seceded, he raised a volunteer company of troops and marched to join the Confederate army in Kentucky.

BRIGADIER GENERAL OTHO STRAHL

1831–1864
Born in Ohio, Stahl eventually moved south. He was a lawyer in Tennessee before joining the Confederate army when the war started.

BRIGADIER GENERAL JOHN CARTER

1837–1864
A former lawyer and university instructor, Carter was mortally wounded during the battle on November 30 and died shortly after.

Brigadier General States Rights Gist   **Brigadier General Otho Strahl**

In 1864, Major General William T. Sherman attacked the South's war-making industries and
its civilian infrastructure. His tactics likely hastened the end of the war, but also left countless
civilians terrorized and homeless.

Sherman, seated at the center of a group of Northern officers, was praised as a military genius by some and as a "lunatic" by others. Despite his controversies, he rose from colonel to commander of all Federal forces in the war's Western Theater.

General William T. Sherman

THE MILITARY LEADER WAS HERALDED FOR HIS BATTLEFIELD WITS BUT HATED FOR HIS HEARTLESS TACTICS.

Like his friend and commander General Grant, Major General William T. Sherman was an Ohio native and a West Pointer. He was a veteran of the Seminole War and, upon its conclusion, accepted a position heading a military academy in Louisiana. When the Civil War broke out, Sherman was offered but declined a Confederate command, and he returned to the U.S. Army.

The erratic, moody Sherman performed well in the First Battle of Bull Run, the first significant battle of the Civil War, and earned the rank of brigadier general. As the war wore on, he was given a command in the Western Theater, then began serving under Grant. Rumors circulated that Sherman was mentally unstable, but Grant continued to increase Sherman's responsibilities, and he distinguished himself at Shiloh, Vicksburg, Chattanooga, and the capture of Atlanta.

While some praised Sherman as a military genius, others condemned him as the "Nero of the 19th Century" for his brutally effective campaign of total war on the March to the Sea and the Carolinas Campaign. As commanding general of the postwar U.S. Army, Sherman would again earn both praise and criticism for defeating the Plains Indians with the slash-and-burn tactics he had unleashed on the South.

In late 1864, General William T. Sherman led an army of 62,000 troops from Atlanta to the coast in what became known as the March to the Sea. The brutal campaign, depicted here in a painting by Felix Octavius Carr Darley, undermined the Southern people's will to resist.

Marching through Georgia

SHERMAN'S SLASH-AND-BURN CAMPAIGN TERRORIZED SOUTHERN CIVILIANS ON THE HOMEFRONT AND SPURRED A WAVE OF DEFECTIONS AMONG CONFEDERATE SOLDIERS.

The goal of his March to the Sea, General William T. Sherman proclaimed, was to "make Georgia howl"—and he did.

For almost one month and 285 miles, Sherman's 62,000-man Army of the Ohio cut a destructive swath across Georgia. Along with military targets, such as 200 miles of railroad, Sherman's troops sacked the state capital at Milledgeville, set fire to sawmills and gristmills, burned countless private homes and barns, and rounded up an estimated 12,000 head of livestock, killing whatever animals they could not eat.

"Saturday morning we looked out upon a scene of desolation and ruin," a Georgia homemaker would later recall. "We could hardly believe it was our home. One week before it was one of the most beautiful places in the state. Now it was a vast wreck."

As a war strategy, the March to the Sea was effective: It terrorized Southern civilians on the home front, spurred a wave of desertion in Lee's army by soldiers determined to go home and protect their families, and proved that the Confederacy could not prevent harm to Southern homes, property, and people.

An illustration shows the devastation left behind by Sherman's army as it moved through Georgia and later the Carolinas. The trail of chimneys from burned homes were dubbed "Sherman's Sentinels" by soldiers and civilians alike.

In this Civil War newspaper illustration, Sherman's "Bummers" looted a Southern plantation

CONFEDERATE ARMY OF MANHATTAN

In November of 1864, following widespread destruction of civilian property in the South by Northern troops, a team of Confederate agents, called the Confederate Army of Manhattan, attempted to retaliate by burning New York City. The conspirators managed to set fires in 13 New York City hotels, on hay barges in New York harbor, and at P.T. Barnum's American Museum. All blazes were extinguished before they spread.

9

1865: A NEW BIRTH OF FREEDOM

AFTER FOUR YEARS AND MORE THAN 620,000 LIVES LOST, THE CIVIL WAR FINALLY
ENDED IN A NORTHERN VICTORY.

On March 4, 1865, President Abraham Lincoln delivered his second inaugural address on the steps of the U.S. Capitol.

"With malice toward none, with charity for all, with firmness in the right as God gives us to see the right, let us . . . bind up the nation's wounds."

—Abraham Lincoln's second inaugural address, March 4, 1865

A lone Northern sentry looks out on the Ogeechee River near Savannah as Union forces mobilize toward South Carolina on the continued March to the Sea.

Sherman Unleashes Total War on South Carolina

THE MAYOR OF COLUMBIA PERSONALLY BEGGED FOR HIS CITY
TO BE SPARED, BUT UNION TROOPS BURNED IT TO RUBBLE.

On January 19, 1865, General William T. Sherman led his victorious army out of Savannah toward South Carolina—the state that many Northerners blamed for starting the war.

"The truth is," Sherman noted, "the whole army is burning with an insatiable desire to wreak vengeance upon South Carolina. I almost tremble for her fate."

South Carolinians had reason to fear: Sherman's troops unleashed the same fury they had on Georgia. "We . . . must make old and young, rich and poor, feel the hard hand of war," Sherman wrote. Entire towns were looted and torched. Livestock and food stores were taken or destroyed on an even greater scale than in Georgia.

"Yesterday we passed the plantation of a Mr. Stubbs," one of Sherman's staff officers reported. "The house, cotton gin, press, corn-ricks, stables, everything that could burn, was in flames."

In February, Sherman's army reached Columbia, South Carolina's capital. The city's mayor Thomas Goodwyn personally begged Sherman to spare it, but that night much of the city was burned to charred rubble. Gangs of drunken Federal troops roamed the streets, setting fire to stores, businesses, and row after row of homes. They destroyed the South Carolina State House, the Methodist church, a Catholic convent, and a priceless museum collection. Sherman blamed the fires on retreating

The Columbia, South Carolina, capitol building stands on February 17, 1865, the day Sherman's troops arrived in the city. It would be in flames by nightfall.

An illustration of Sherman's troops marching through South Carolina. "I almost tremble for her fate," the general said of the Palmetto State.

Confederate cavalrymen, but eyewitnesses told a different story: "The city of Columbia, S.C. was burned by a drunken mob," reported a Northern officer.

Morale in South Carolina Crumbles

From Columbia, Sherman's columns moved northward, continuing their destruction until they reached North Carolina. There, the troops were brought under control and destruction of civilian property was curtailed. Although controversial, Sherman's brutal tactics in South Carolina proved as effective as they did in Georgia: civilian morale plummeted, and more Southern troops slipped away from the ranks to return home to protect their families.

1865

January

The War Comes to an End

The Union's major victories forced Lee's surrender.

January 19 General William T. Sherman launches his Carolinas Campaign.

February 17 Columbia, South Carolina is burned while occupied by Sherman's army.

March 4 President Abraham Lincoln was inaugurated for a second term.

April 9 Lee surrenders to Grant at Appomattox.

April

April 14 President Abraham Lincoln was assassinated at Ford's Theatre by John Wilkes Booth, a disgruntled Confederate sympathizer.

April 26 Confederate Army of Tennessee surrenders.

May 10 Confederate president Jefferson Davis was arrested in Georgia.

May 10 Andrew Johnson, who succeeded Abraham Lincoln as president, declared hostilities are ended.

May 12 Last battle of the Civil War occurred at Palmito Ranch in Texas.

August

May 22 Confederate president Jefferson Davis was imprisoned at Fort Monroe.

December 18 Thirteenth Amendment to the U.S. Constitution is ratified ending slavery in America.

December

Columbia, South Carolina's once graceful capital, was gutted by Sherman's army. "Go home and rest assured that your city will be as safe in my hands as if you controlled it," Sherman told the town's mayor.

South Carolina's statehouse was destroyed by Sherman's army in February 1865, but after the South surrendered, construction on its replacement began.

WITNESS TO WAR

Hell on Earth

COLUMBIA, SOUTH CAROLINA BURNED AT THE HAND OF THE UNION ARMY.

As they marched into Columbia on February 17, 1865, Sherman's soldiers sang a perverted version of the patriotic song "Hail, Columbia," which was regarded as one of a few unofficial national anthems at the time. The troops' revised lyrics: "Hail Columbia, Happy land. If I don't burn you, I'll be damned." The torching of South Carolina's capital city became one of the greatest controversies of the Civil War. For residents of the city, the event was "hell on earth," as described by a Columbia survivor in a letter to her daughter.

Columbia, March 3, 1865

My Dear Gracia:

Doubtless your anxiety is very great to hear something about us after the great calamity that has befallen our town. We have lost everything, but thank God, our lives have been spared. Oh Gracia, what we have passed through no tongue can tell, it defies description! Such a scene as was witnessed on the day and night of 17 February. God grant that we may never see the like again!

The enemy entered the city about nine o'clock in the morning; passed our street about ten, and at dark were still passing. . . . The first thing they did was break open the stores and distribute the goods right and left. They found liquor and all became heartily drunk. The very elements seemed to conspire against us, for the wind blew a perfect gale. Bags of cotton were cut open in the streets and the wind carried it even into the trees. The streets looked as if they were covered with snow. When night came on, the soldiers went about with matches, turpentine and cotton, with which they fired the houses. It was a fearful sight, in whatever direction your eyes, they met the flaming fire. At one time I thought there was no way of escape left for us . . . While I was getting some things out of a trunk there were three men in the room rifling another, but I felt no fear, tho alone. One Yankee was burned to death on our own lot. I can compare that night to nothing but hell on earth. . . .

We stayed all night in the street, protected by a Yankee captain from Iowa who was very kind to us. . . . We have two rooms on the first floor of the [Lutheran] seminary. What we are to do for clothes I know not, but God will provide. Rich and poor are drawing rations alike. There is not a house left on Marion Street. . . .

Your ever affectionate
Mother

THE FACE OF WAR
THE TOLL OF OFFICE

When Abraham Lincoln ran for the presidency in 1860, he was 51 years old. Four and a half years later, the weight of the war was visible on his face.

1860

1865

ABOVE: Following the ratification of the Thirteenth Amendment, some slaves would be allowed to own their own land. OPPOSITE RIGHT: Though freedom brought widespread rejoicing for America's former slaves, as seen in this artwork, it also brought new challenges. Most former slaves remained in the South and, lacking resources to strike out on their own, many became dependent on white landowners through sharecropping, a system which often became exploitative.

The Thirteenth Amendment Ends Slavery in America

THE RATIFICATION PROCESS TOOK A YEAR, AND SOME STATES ONLY AGREED WHEN FORCED BY CONGRESS.

"Neither slavery nor involuntary servitude . . . shall exist within the United States. . . ." So read the Thirteenth Amendment to the United States Constitution, introduced in early 1864 by Missouri congressman John Henderson.

Turning the amendment into law was not easy. Northern Democrats, who believed the legality of slavery was up to the states, not Congress, sought to corral opposition in the legislature. President Lincoln and Secretary of State William Seward counter-maneuvered. Once the amendment was passed by Congress on January 31, 1865 it still had to be sent to state legislatures to be ratified. Three-quarters of the state bodies had to approve, which at the time added up to 27 states.

It took almost a full year for state legislatures to ratify the amendment, and some only did so under duress. While most Northern states supported ratification, those in the South resisted. Congress forced the issue by requiring the states to approve the Thirteenth Amendment in order to be readmitted to the Union. Finally, on December 6, 1865, Georgia became the 27th state to do so. Slavery in the United States was officially outlawed.

LEFT: The end of slavery in America signaled a new beginning for former slaves, but one that came with many challenges. Without food, shelter, and education many freed slaves needed assistance from agencies such as the Relief of Freedom and Refugees. ABOVE: Following the Emancipation Proclamation, freed slaves often found themselves doing the same work they had under the plantation system.

In spite of an overnight rainstorm that soaked Washington, D.C., a large crowd gathered outside the capitol on March 4, 1865, to hear President Lincoln deliver his second inaugural address.

GENERAL ANDERSON RETURNS TO FORT SUMTER

In a ceremony at Fort Sumter on April 14, 1865, Brigadier General Robert Anderson, the U.S. Army major who surrendered the fort in hopes of avoiding conflict, victoriously raised the U.S. flag above the fort's battered walls. The flag raising at Fort Sumter occurred four years from the day that it was lowered in surrender—the event that ignited the Civil War.

Lincoln's Second Inauguration

THE PRESIDENT CALLED FOR
"MALICE TOWARD NONE."

On March 4, 1865, President Abraham Lincoln was inaugurated for a second term in Washington, D.C., this time as the commander in chief who had led the North to an almost certain victory.

A large and enthusiastic crowd tromped through streets muddied by an overnight rainstorm to stand beneath the U.S. Capitol's new dome and hear Lincoln's address. "The fears of the olden times were forgotten," a newspaper reported. "Happy faces and cheerful greetings were everywhere observed."

In his speech, Lincoln encouraged citizens to put the divisions of war behind them. "Fondly do we hope—fervently do we pray—that this mighty scourge of war may speedily pass away," he said, calling for reconciliation. "With malice toward none; with charity toward all," he said, "let us . . . bind up the nation's wounds. . . ."

At the completion of the ceremony, Lincoln lifted the Bible on which he had taken the oath of office and pressed it to his lips. In barely a month, General Robert E. Lee would surrender his army in Appomattox, Virginia, signaling an end to the Civil War.

This image was taken in early 1865 by Alexander Gardner; it marked one of the last times President Abraham Lincoln posed for a photographer before he was assassinated.

Accompanied by a seemingly endless line of supply wagons, victorious troops from the Army of the Potomac entered Petersburg.

The End Is Near

WHEN A SOUTHERN GENERAL LEFT HIS LINE FOR A FISH FRY NEAR PETERSBURG,
THE UNION LAUNCHED AN ATTACK THAT WOULD HELP TOPPLE RICHMOND.

After a ten-month siege at Petersburg, where Grant used the Army of the Potomac to stretch Southern troops thinner and thinner, Union soldiers finally broke through the Confederate line.

It started at a crossroads called Five Forks when Grant ordered the cavalry to attack a weakened section of Lee's line. The sector was defended by troops under General George Pickett, known for his heroic charge at the Battle of Gettysburg. Lee instructed Pickett to "hold Five Forks at all hazards," but on April 1, Pickett briefly left his station to share in a shad bake with other Southern officers.

The fish fry gave the North the opening it needed and General Philip Sheridan launched the attack. Before daylight Grant had ordered a general assault on Lee's lines at Petersburg. His long, arduous siege was over.

Lee's army was forced into retreat and members of the Confederate government evacuated Richmond on Sunday, April 2, 1865. Richmond's citizens also fled, and warehouses of military supplies were set afire by retreating Southern troops. An eyewitness described the chaotic scene: "a column of white smoke rose up as high as the eye could reach, instantaneously followed by a deafening sound. The earth seemed to rock and tremble

ABOVE: When Lee's defensive line at Petersburg collapsed, the Confederate capital of Richmond could no longer be defended. Confederate officials evacuated the city and the army set fire to military stores—causing a blaze that ravaged much of the city.

Even heavy artillery was not enough to hold off the Union attack on Petersburg. On April 2, 1865, Lee's army was forced to retreat.

as with the shock of an earthquake. . . ." After four years of warfare and stubborn resistance, Richmond was occupied by Northern troops.

Lee led his battered Army of Northern Virginia on a march for the railroad at Danville, Virginia, with Grant's 60,000-man army in determined pursuit. The Southern general's remaining gamble was to unite his depleted army with Confederate General Joseph E. Johnston's army, which was trying to hold off Sherman's Federal army in North Carolina.

It was not to be. As Lee withdrew across southern Virginia, he suffered a devastating defeat at the Battle of Sayler's Creek on April 6, 1865. There, more than one-fourth of his 30,000 troops were captured by Federal forces. Lee personally rallied the remnants of his army, and resumed his path westward. It would be the last march for the Army of Northern Virginia.

GENERAL JOSEPH E. JOHNSTON
1807–1891

When Joseph E. Johnston joined the Confederacy, he was one of the highest-ranking military men to leave Union forces. Johnston had served as a second lieutenant in the army and as a quartermaster general during the Mexican-American War. With his experience, he became a senior officer and general in the Southern army. Johnston led successful battles early on in the war, including a victory in the First Battle of Bull Run. But he soon came under criticism for inadequate offensive strategy and was replaced by Robert E. Lee as commander of the Army of Northern Virginia in 1862. Johnston later commanded troops fighting against Union forces marching from Chattanooga to Atlanta, but ultimately surrendered to General William T. Sherman in April 1865 in the largest surrender of the war.

Lee led his depleted army in a retreat from Petersburg, hoping to regroup and continue to fight, but his march was blocked near the Virginia hamlet of Appomattox Court House. There, on April 9, 1865, Lee surrendered to Grant, triggering an end to the Civil War.

Surrender at Appomattox

LEE, SURROUNDED AND SEVERELY OUTNUMBERED, SURRENDERED TO GRANT.
THE UNION GENERAL OFFERED AID AND MERCY TO THE CONFEDERATE TROOPS.

It was Palm Sunday, April 9, 1865. Lee's Army of Northern Virginia, now skeletal thin with little more than 20,000 troops, was being pursued by Grant with an army five times that size. After beating back Northern cavalry near the community of Appomattox Court House in southwest Virginia, the Confederates resumed their retreat when they came to a phalanx of blue-uniformed Northern infantry.

Poised defiantly under red, unfurled battle standards, Lee's army steeled itself as the Federal troops prepared to make a death attack. Then a lone Confederate horseman emerged from the Southern lines, bearing a white flag. General Lee was ready to meet with General Grant.

That afternoon the two commanders and their staff officers convened in the parlor of a two-story brick farmhouse near the courthouse at Appomattox. One of Lee's officers urged him not to surrender, but to turn the army lose in the Appalachian Mountains to wage guerilla war. Lee would not hear of it: he and his army had fought honorably, and they would surrender honorably.

Compelled to Yield

Lee was immaculately uniformed; Grant was rumpled, "dusty and a little soiled" from being in the field, an officer noticed. The two had many common acquaintances—Lee had once headed West Point—and they had both served in the Mexican-American War. They briefly exchanged small talk, then Lee moved the conversation to the reason for their meeting.

Grant offered generous terms: Lee's troops could

Grant and Lee met to discuss surrender terms at the home of Wilmer McLean, a Virginia farmer who had moved to Appomattox from Manassas to escape the war.

Upon hearing of Lee's surrender, General Joseph Johnston surrendered his Confederate army to General William T. Sherman in North Carolina after negotiations in this Durham farmhouse

Mathew Brady photographed General Robert E. Lee with his eldest son Major General George Washington Custis Lee, left, and Colonel Walter Taylor, right, following the surrender.

As depicted in this sketch by an eyewitness, Lee rode through the ranks of his army after surrendering. He was enveloped by his soldiers. Some wept. Others just silently removed their hats. "I love you just as well as ever, General Lee," one yelled.

go home—no prison camps. Officers could keep their sidearms, cavalrymen could keep their horses, and the half-starved Southerners would be issued rations by the Northern victors. Then it was done, and Lee slowly rode away. He issued General Order Number Nine to his troops: "After four years of arduous service marked by unsurpassed courage and fortitude, the Army of Northern Virginia has been compelled to yield to overwhelming numbers and resources. . . . I earnestly pray that a Merciful God will extend to you his blessing and protection."

When Northern artillery began firing celebratory salutes, Grant ordered it stopped. "We did not want to exult over their downfall," he later explained. From North Carolina to Texas, Southern commanders one by one followed Lee's example, and laid down arms. After four years of warfare, the fighting had finally ended.

After Lincoln's assassination in Washington, D.C., a special train, right, carried his body to mourning events along a 1,654-mile route that included stops in Baltimore, Philadelphia, New York City, and Columbus. In Chicago, left, 7,000 people an hour viewed his body.

The nation mourned as Lincoln's funeral procession made its way through the East. Here crowds in New York City's Union Square gathered as the procession approached.

Tragedy at Ford's Theatre

A DISGRUNTLED SON OF THE SOUTH ASSASSINATED ABRAHAM LINCOLN.

A week after Appomattox, President Abraham Lincoln gave an impromptu speech to a crowd that gathered on the White House lawn to mark the end of America's bloodiest war. Lincoln asked a band to play "Dixie," signaling his intention to restore the South back into the Union with easy terms. A week later, he was dead—assassinated while attending a play in Washington, D.C.

It was the evening of April 14, 1865, Good Friday. Lincoln and the First Lady had gone to Ford's Theatre to see the English farce, "Our American Cousin." While Lincoln's sole bodyguard was absent, actor John Wilkes Booth, embittered by the defeat of the South, slipped into the presidential box. He shot the president in the rear of the head with a .44 caliber derringer, then escaped, only to be cornered 12 days later and killed by Federal troops.

Lincoln was carried across the street to the Petersen House, the private home of William and Anna Petersen, where he died early the next morning.

On the evening of April 14, 1865, President Lincoln was mortally wounded while attending a play, *Our American Cousin*, at Ford's Theater in Washington, D.C.

After a funeral in the East Room of the White House, Lincoln's body was escorted in a military procession along Pennsylvania Avenue to the U.S. Capitol, where it lay in state in the Capitol Rotunda until carried by a special train to Springfield, Illinois for burial.

John Wilkes Booth, a well-known American actor, gained entrance to Ford's Theater and shot Lincoln from behind while he was watching the play. Booth was later killed by Federal troops.

After a military trial, four convicted conspirators in the Lincoln assassination were hanged on July 7, 1865.

Seventy-five years after the Battle of Gettysburg, two Civil War veterans—one Southern, one Northern—clasped hands as friends at the once-bloodied wall on Cemetery Ridge.

A Just and Lasting Peace

A FRACTURED NATION
BEGAN TO HEAL.

At the end of the first day's fighting at Gettysburg, Lieutenant Colonel John R. Lane of North Carolina was hit in the back of the neck by a .58 caliber bullet. Lane went down, an eyewitness reported, "as limber as a rag" and presumably dead. The bullet was fired by a Northern soldier from Michigan—Corporal Charles McConnell— who would always remember how he steadied his rifle against a tree and shot down the tall Southern officer. Miraculously, Lane survived his wound and the war.

Decades later, the two former enemies were introduced at a postwar veterans' event. Although they had fought hard and done their best to kill each other in battle, Lane and McConnell became close friends. In 1903, on the 40th anniversary of Gettysburg, they made a joint appearance at ceremonies on the battlefield. As a crowd of several thousand applauded, McConnell told Lane, "I thank God I did not kill you."

Their experience was remarkable, but it was not unique. Despite four years of unprecedented bloodletting, the soldiers of the Civil War were Americans—and in the decades that followed the Civil War, they led the nation in an extraordinary healing process.

TOP: A lithograph published at war's end portrayed a soldier returning from the war being embraced by his family. BOTTOM LEFT: So many on both sides never returned home—more than 620,000. The soldiers' section of Richmond's Oakwood Cemetery contained more than 17,000 graves. BOTTOM RIGHT: The war left widespread destruction and poverty in its wake in the South. Full recovery would require generations of effort.

Brigadier General Joshua Chamberlain described the actual surrender of Lee's army at Appomattox to *Harper's Weekly* artist John R. Chapin, who detailed the event in this sketch. After battling each other for more than three years, the armies ended the war with a mutual salute.

At Appomattox, General Joshua Lawrence Chamberlain was given the honor of overseeing the surrender of Lee's army. He ordered Northern troops to salute the surrendering Southern soldiers as their returning countrymen.

Confederate Brigadier General John B. Gordon led Lee's troops to the surrender site at Appomattox, and led the Southern soldiers in returning the Northern troops' salute.

It was, perhaps, an unlikely recovery from a war that claimed more than 620,000 lives and a Reconstruction Era marred by inequities. Unlike civil wars that had ravaged other countries and often lead to renewed fighting, the American Civil War was followed by an extraordinary national reconciliation—led in no small way by the former soldiers in blue and gray.

General Ulysses S. Grant set the tone when he granted generous surrender terms at Appomattox. So did General Robert E. Lee when he kept his defeated troops from resorting to guerilla warfare at war's end.

Northern General Joshua Lawrence Chamberlain, assigned to oversee Lee's troops as they stacked their arms at Appomattox, insisted his men maintain a respectful silence during the ceremony. When the Southern soldiers came alongside, he ordered Northerners to assume the position of "carry arms," a military salute of respect. Surprised, Lee's troops responded by returning the gesture, thus ending the Civil War with the former foes saluting each other as Americans all.

To be sure, there was lingering bitterness and divisions across the country. There would be injustices for generations to come. But many veterans found a bond in their service. Some even began holding joint reunions on the old battlefields, greeting each other as "my friend the enemy." They shook hands, swapped stories, and helped the nation begin to heal.

At the end of the war in May 1865 more than 150,000 victorious Northern troops paraded down Pennsylvania Avenue in Washington, D.C. in what was proclaimed as the Grand Review. Afterwards, all Federal volunteer troops were discharged to return to civilian life.

In the years following the war, William T. Sherman remained active in the veterans' community, where he was a highly regarded speaker. He appears here, in the center of the front row, along with Union soldiers.

Under the gaze of their white Northern schoolteachers, former slaves assembled outside their first schoolhouse on South Carolina's St. Helena Island. Freedom brought opportunities for education, but the nation had a long way to go to provide equality for people of color.

LEFT: Captured by Northern troops after the fall of Richmond, Confederate President Jefferson Davis was shackled and imprisoned without trial at Fort Monroe, Virginia for two years. Eventually, Federal authorities decided not to prosecute former Confederate leaders, and freed Davis and others. RIGHT: Jefferson Davis wrote *A Short History of the Confederate States of America* shortly before his death in December 1889.

In 1901, the U.S. Congress authorized a massive monument to General Grant in front of the U.S. Capitol, and two decades later it was officially dedicated.

In Baltimore, Maryland, a monument was built to honor common Confederate soldiers. Similar statues were erected throughout the country.

At the 50th anniversary of the Battle of Gettysburg in 1913, an elderly Confederate soldier shook hands with an aging Union veteran.

INDEX

SELECTED BIBLIOGRAPHY

Akerman, Robert K. *Wade Hampton III.* Columbia: University of South Carolina Press, 2007.

Aldrich, Thomas M. *The History of Battery A, First Regiment Rhode Island Light Artillery.* Providence: Snow and Farnham, 1904.

Alexander, Edward Porter. *Fighting for the Confederacy: The Personal Recollections of General Edward Porter Alexander.* Gary W. Gallagher, editor. Chapel Hill: University of North Carolina Press, 1989.

Alleman, Tillie Pierce. *At Gettysburg: Or, What a Girl Heard and Saw at the Battle.* New York: Lake Borland, 1889.

American Heroism: As Told by the Medal Winners and Roll of Honor Men. Springfield: J.W. Jones, 1897.

Annals of the War: Written by Leading Participants North and South. Alexander K. McClure, editor. Philadelphia: Times Publishing, 1879.

Bachelder Papers: Gettysburg in Their Own Words. David Ladd and Audrey Ladd, editors. Dayton: Morningside, 1994–1995.

Barlow, Francis C. *"Fear Was Not in Him": The Civil War Letters of Francis C. Barlow.* Christian G. Samito, editor. New York: Fordham University Press, 2004.

Barrett, John G. *Sherman's March through the Carolinas.* Chapel Hill: University of North Carolina Press, 1956.

Battles and Leaders of the Civil War. Robert Underwood Johnson and Clarence Clough Buel, editors. New York: Thomas Yoseloff, 1956.

Blackford, W.W. *War Years with Jeb Stuart.* New York: Charles Scribner's Sons, 1945.

Blaine, James G. *Twenty Years of Congress: From Lincoln to Garfield.* Norwich: Henry Bill, 1884.

The Blue and the Gray: The Story of the Civil War as Told by Participants. Henry Steele Commager, editor. New York: Fairfax Press, 1982.

Boatner, Mark Mayo, III. *The Civil War Dictionary.* New York: David McKay, 1959.

Brown, J. Willard. *The Signal Corps, USA, in the War of the Rebellion.* Boston: U.S. Veterans Signal Corps Association, 1896.

Busey, John W. and David G. Martin. *Regimental Strengths and Losses at Gettysburg.* Hightstown: Longstreet House, 1994.

Cannon, Devereaux, Jr. *The Flags of the Confederacy: An Illustrated History.* Memphis: St. Luke's Press, 1988.

Chamberlain, Joshua Lawrence. *The Passing of the Armies: An Account of the Final Campaign of the Army of the Potomac.* New York: G.P. Putnam, 1915.

Chambers, Bruce W. *Art and Artists of the South.* Columbia, S.C.: University of South Carolina Press, 1984.

Cheesebrough, David. *Oratory from Slavery: Frederick Douglass.* Westport: Greenwood Press, 1998.

Chestnut, Mary Boykin. *A Diary from Dixie.* Isabella D. Martin and Myrta Lockett Avary, editors. New York: D. Appleton, 1905.

Civil War Naval Chronology, 1861-1865. Washington, D.C.: U.S. Government Printing Office, 1971.

Cleutz, David. *Fields of Fame and Glory: Col. David Ireland and the 137th New York State Volunteers.* Bloomington: Xlibris, 2010.

Coddington, Edwin B. *The Gettysburg Campaign: A Study in Command.* New York: Charles Scribner's Sons, 1963.

Coffin, Charles Carlton. *Four Years of Fighting: A Volume of Personal Observations with the Army and the Navy.* Boston: Ticknor and Fields, 1866.

Coffin, Howard. *Nine Months to Gettysburg: Stannard's Vermonters and the Repulse of Pickett's Charge.* Woodstock: Countryman, 1997.

Collected Works of Abraham Lincoln. Roy P. Basler, editor. New Brunswick: Rutgers University Press, 1953.

Cooke, John Esten. *Wearing of the Gray: Being Personal Portraits, Scenes and Adventures of the War.* New York: E.B. Treat, 1867.

Crawford, Richard. *The Civil War Songbook.* New York: Dover Publications, 1977.

Cumming, Kate. *A Journal of Hospital Life in the Confederate Army of Tennessee.* Louisville: John P. Morton, 1866.

Davis, Jefferson. *The Papers of Jefferson Davis and the Confederacy, Including Diplomatic Correspondence, 1861-1865.* James D. Richardson and Alan Nevins, editors. New York: Chelsea House, 1966.

Dawes, Rufus. *Service with the Sixth Wisconsin Volunteers.* Marietta: Alderman & Sons, 1890.

Dyer, Frederick H. *A Compendium of the War of the Rebellion.* New York: Thomas Yoseloff, 1959.

Eggleston, George Cary. *A Rebel's Recollections.* New York: G.P. Putnam, 1878.

Encyclopedia of the Civil War: A Political, Social, and Military History. David S. Heidler and Jeanne T. Heidler, editors. New York: W.W. Norton, 2000.

Encyclopedia of the Confederacy. Richard N. Current, editor. New York: Simon & Schuster, 1993.

Evans, Robley D. *A Sailor's Log: Recollections of Forty Years of Naval Life.* New York: D. Appleton, 1908.

Fisher (John) Papers. *Civil War Times Illustrated Collection.* Archives Branch, U.S. Army Military History Institute.

Fleming, George T. *The Life and Letters of Alexander Hays.* Pittsburgh: 1919.

Forbes, Edwin. *Thirty Years After: An Artist's Memoir of the Civil War.* New York: Fords, Howard & Hulbert, 1890.

Fox, William F. *Regimental Losses in the American Civil War, 1861-1865.* Albany: Randow, 1889.

Freeman, Douglas Southall. *Lee's Lieutenants: A Study in Command.* New York: Charles Scribner's Sons, 1944.

Fremantle, Arthur Lyon. *Three Months in the Southern States.* Mobile: S.H. Goetzel, 1864.

Frye, Rose. "The Way We Lived Then." *Our Women in the War.* Charleston: News and Courier Press, 1885.

Fuller, J.F.C. *The Conduct of War: 1789-1961.* New Brunswick: Rutgers University Press, 1961.

Gallagher, Gary W. *Chancellorsville: The Battle and Its Aftermath.* Chapel Hill: University of North Carolina Press, 1996.

Gardner, Alexander. *Photographic Sketchbook of the War.* Mineola: Dover, 1959.

Gaston (David) Papers. Harrisburg Civil War Roundtable Collection. Archives Branch. U.S. Army Military History Collection.

Gibbon, John. *Personal Recollections of the Civil War.* New York: G.P. Putnam's Sons, 1928.

Gordon, John B. *Reminiscences of the Civil War.* New York: Charles Scribner's Sons, 1903.

Gorham, George C. *Life and Public Services of Edwin M. Stanton.* Boston: Houghton Mifflin, 1899.

Gottfried, Bradley M. *The Brigades of Gettysburg: The Union and Confederate Brigades at the Battle of Gettysburg.* Cambridge: DaCapo Press, 2003.

Washington, D.C.: Regnery History, 2012.

Hancock, Almira Russell. *Reminiscences of Winfield Scott Hancock by His Wife.* New York: Charles L. Webster, 1887.

Hancock, Cornelia. *Letters of a Civil War Nurse.* Henrietta S. Jaquette, editor. Lincoln: Bison Books, 1998.

Hanna, Charles W. *African American recipients of the Medal of Honor.* Jefferson: McFarland Publishing, 2002.

Haskell, Frank Aretas. *The Battle of Gettysburg.* Bruce Catton, editor. Boston: Houghton Mifflin, 1958.

Hattaway, Herman. *Shades of Blue and Gray.* Columbia: University of Missouri Press, 1997.

Hebert, Walter H. *Fighting Joe Hooker.* Indianapolis: Bobbs-Merrill, 1944.

Hess, Earl J. *Pickett's Charge: The Last Attack at Gettysburg.* Chapel Hill: University of North Carolina Press, 2001.

Heth, Henry. *The Memoir of Henry Heth.* James L. Morrison Jr., editor. Westport: Greenwood Press, 1974.

Historical Times Illustrated History of the Civil War. Patricia Faust, editor. New York: Harper & Row, 1986.

Hoehling, A.A. *Vicksburg: 47 Days of Siege.* Mechanicsburg: Stackpole Books, 1996.

Hoke, Jacob. *The Great Invasion of 1863.* Dayton: W.J. Shuey, 1887.

Holt, David E. *A Mississippi Rebel in the Army of Northern Virginia.* Thomas D. Cockrell and Michael B. Ballard, editors. Baton Rouge: LSU Press, 1995.

Holt (David Eldred) Papers. Manuscripts Collection. Mississippi Department of Archives and History.

Hood, John Bell. *Advance and Retreat: Personal Experiences in the United States and Confederate States Armies.* New Orleans: G.T. Beauregard, 1880.

Hoke, Jacob. *The Great Invasion.* Dayton: W.J. Shuey, 1887.

Hoisington, Daniel J. *Gettysburg and the Christian Commission,* Brunswick: Edinborough Press, 2002.

Hunter, Alexander. "A High Private's Account of the Battle of Sharpsburg," *Southern Historical Society Papers* 10 (October/November 1882).

Johnston, John White. *The True Story of "Jennie" Wade.* Rochester: Johnston, 1917.

Jones, J. William. *Christ in the Camp: Or, Religion in Lee's Army.* Richmond: B.F. Johnson, 1888.

Jones, Terry L. *Lee's Tigers: The Louisiana Infantry in the Army of Northern Virginia.* Baton Rouge: LSU Press, 1987.

Kidd, James Harvey. *Personal Recollections of a Cavalryman with Custer's Michigan Cavalry Brigade in the Civil War.* Ionia, MI: Sentinel, 1908.

The Library of Congress Civil War Desk Reference. Margaret E. Wagner, Gary Gallagher, Paul Finkelman, editors. New York: Simon & Schuster, 2002.

Lincoln, Abraham. *The Collected Works of Abraham Lincoln.* Roy Prentice Basler, editor. New Brunswick: Rutgers University Press, 1953.

Long, E.B. *The Civil War Day by Day: An Almanac 1861–1865.* Garden City: Doubleday, 1971.

Longacre, Edward G. *General John: A Military Biography.* Cambridge: De Capo, 1995.

Longstreet, James. *From Manassas to Appomattox: Memoirs of the Civil War in America.* Philadelphia: J.B. Lippincott, 1908.

McClellan, Henry B. *The Life and Campaigns of Major General J.E.B. Stuart.* Boston: Houghton Mifflin, 1885.

McPherson, James M. *Battle Cry of Freedom: The Civil War Era.* Oxford: Oxford University Press, 1988.

Meade, George. *The Life and Letters of George Gordon Meade.* George Gordon Meade, editor. New York: Charles Scribner's Sons, 1913.

Moe, Richard. *The Last Full Measure: The Life and Death of the First Minnesota Volunteers.* New York: Henry Holt, 1993.

Moffett, George H. "War Prison Experience." *Confederate Veteran* 13, no. 4 (April 1876).

Neese, George M. *Three Years in the Confederate Horse Artillery.* New York: Neale Publishing, 1911.

Nolan, Alan T. *The Iron Brigade: A Military History.* New York: Macmillan, 1961.

Oates, William C. "Gettysburg: The Battle on the Right." *Southern Historical Society Papers* 6 (1878).

Perrett, Thomas. "A Trip that Didn't Pay." Thomas Perrett Papers. North Carolina Department of Archives and History.

Pickett, George Edward and La Salle Corbell Pickett. *The Heart of a Soldier: As Revealed in the Intimate Letters of George E. Pickett.* New York: Seth Moye, 1913.

Porter, David D. *Incidents and Anecdotes of the Civil War.* New York: D. Appleton, 1885.

Randall, J.G. and David Donald. *The Civil War and Reconstruction.* Boston: D.C. Heath, 1961.

Reed, Charles W. *A Grand Terrible Drama: The Civil War Letters of Charles Wellington Reed.* Eric Campbell, editor. New York: Fordham University Press, 2000.

Reidy, Joseph P. "Black Men in Blue during the Civil War." *Prologue Magazine* 3, no. 3 (Fall 2001).

Robertson, James I., Jr. *General A.P. Hill: The Story of a Confederate Warrior.* New York: Random House, 1987.

Schaff, Morris. *The Battle of the Wilderness.* Boston: Houghton Mifflin, 1910.

Schurz, Carl. *The Reminiscences of Carl Schurz.* Garden City, NY: Doubleday, Page & Company, 1917.

Sears, Stephen W. *Gettysburg.* New York: Houghton Mifflin, 2003.

Sherman, William T. *Sherman's Civil War: Selected Correspondence of William T. Sherman, 1860-1865.* Jean V. Berlin and Brooks D. Simpson, editors. Chapel Hill: University of North Carolina Press, 1999.

Smith, Derek. *The Gallant Dead: Union and Confederate Generals Killed in the Civil War.* Mechanicsburg: Stackpole, 2005.

Sorrell, G. Moxley. *Recollections of a Confederate Staff Officer.* New York: Neale Publishing, 1905.

Sterling, Dorothy. *The Making of an Afro-American: Martin Robinson Delany.* New York: De Capo Press, 1996.

Stickley, Ezra E. "Wounded at Sharpsburg." *Confederate Veteran* 25, no. 1. (January 1917).

Stiles, Robert. *Four Years under Marse Robert.* New York: Neale Publishing, 1910.

Stine, James Henry. *A History of the Army of the Potomac.* Washington, D.C.: Gibson Brothers, 1893.

Tagg, Larry. *The Unpopular Mr. Lincoln: The Story of America's Most Reviled President.* New York: Savas Beatie, 2009.

Taylor, Walter H. *Four Years with General Lee.* New York: D. Appleton, 1878.

Trudeau, Noah Andre. *Gettysburg: A Testing of Courage.* New York: HarperCollins, 2002.

Trulock, Alice Rains. *In the Hands of Providence: Joshua Chamberlain and the American Civil War.* Chapel Hill: University of North Carolina Press, 1992.

Tucker, Glenn. *High Tide at Gettysburg,* Gettysburg: Stan Clark Military Books, 1995.

War of the Rebellion: The Official Records of the Union and Confederate Armies. Washington, D.C.: Official Government Printing Office, 1880-1901.

Warner, Ezra J. *Generals in Blue: Lives of Union Commanders.* Baton Rouge: LSU Press, 1964.

Watkins, Samuel R. *Co. Aytch.* Jackson: McCowat-Mercer Press, 1952.

Wert, Jeffry D. *Cavalryman of the Lost Cause: A Biography of J.E.B. Stuart.* New York: Simon and Schuster, 2003.

White, Ronald C. *Lincoln's Greatest Speech: The Second Inaugural.* New York: Simon and Schuster, 2003.

Wightman, Edward K. *From Antietam to Fort Fisher: The Letters of Edward King Wightman, 1862-1865.* Edward G. Longacre, editor. Cranbury: Associated University Presses, 1985.

Wiley, Bell I. *The Life of Billy Yank: The Common Soldier of the Union.* Baton Rouge: LSU Press, 1978.

Wilson, Clyde N. *Carolina Cavalier: The Life and Mind of James Johnston Pettigrew.* Athens: University of Georgia Press, 1990.

Wise, Jennings Cropper. *The Long Arm of Lee: The History of the Artillery of the Army of Northern Virginia.* Lincoln: University of Nebraska Press, 1991.

Wittenmyer, Elizabeth. *Queen of the Confederacy: The Innocent Deceits of Lucy Holcombe Pickens.* Denton: University of North Texas Press, 2010.

Woodworth, Steven E. *Beneath a Northern Sky: A Short History of the Gettysburg Campaign.* Lanham: Rowman & Littlefield, 2008.

Worsham, John H. *One of Jackson's Foot Cavalry.* New York: Neale, 1912.

Wyeth, John Allan. *That Devil Forrest: The Life of General Nathan Bedford Forrest.* Baton Rouge: LSU Press, 1989.

IMAGE CREDITS

FRONT COVER
Courtesy Library of Congress; Time Life Pictures/
US Army/National Archives/The LIFE Picture
Collection/Getty Images; Courtesy Library
of Congress; Archive Photos/Getty Images;
Courtesy Library of Congress; MPI/Getty Images

BACK COVER
Courtesy Library of Congress; Courtesy Library of
Congress; Omikron Omikron/Getty Images

p. 2: Top Left: Courtesy Library of Congress
p.2 Top Right: © Corbis p.2 Middle: Courtesy
Library of Congress p.2 Bottom: Courtesy Library
of Congress p. 3: Top Left: Courtesy Library of
Congress p. 3: Top Middle Left: Courtesy Library
of Congress p. 3: Middle Left: Courtesy Library
of Congress p. 3: Bottom Middle Left: Courtesy
National Archives and Records Administration p.
3: Bottom Left: Courtesy National Archives and
Records Administration p. 3: Top Right: Courtesy
National Archives and Records Administration p.
3: Top Middle Right: MPI / Stringer p. 3: Middle
Right: Courtesy Library of Congress p. 3: Bottom
Middle Right: Courtesy Library of Congress p. 3:
Bottom Right: Courtesy Library of Congress p. 4:
Time Life Pictures/US Army/National Archives/
The LIFE Picture Collection/Getty Images

1: A GROWING FISSURE
pp. 6–7: Courtesy Library of Congress p. 8: Left:
Fotosearch/Getty Images p. 8: Right: Fotosearch/
Getty Images p. 9: Top Right: Courtesy Library
of Congress p. 9: Bottom: Courtesy Library of
Congress p. 10: Top Left: William England/
London Stereoscopic Company/Getty Images p.
10: Top Right: Hulton Archive/Getty Images p.
10: Middle Left: Courtesy Library of Congress p.
10: Middle Right: Courtesy Library of Congress
p. 10: Bottom Left: Courtesy Library of Congress
p. 10: Bottom Right: MPI/Getty Images p. 11:
Top: Kean Collection/Getty Images p. 11: Middle:
Kean Collection/Getty Images p. 11: Bottom:
Universal History Archive/UIG via Getty Images
p. 12: Top: Courtesy Library of Congress p. 13:
Left: Fotosearch/Getty Images p. 13: Top Right:
Courtesy Library of Congress p. 13: Bottom Right:
Courtesy Library of Congress p. 14: Top Left:
Courtesy Library of Congress p. 14: Top Right:
Courtesy Library of Congress p. 14: Bottom Left:
Courtesy Library of Congress p. 14: Bottom
Middle: Samuel N. Fox/George Eastman House/
Getty Images p. 14: Bottom Right: Ann Ronan
Pictures/Print Collector/Getty Images p. 15: Top
Left: Courtesy Library of Congress p. 15: Top
Right: Courtesy Library of Congress p. 15: Bottom
Left: Courtesy Library of Congress p. 15: Bottom
Right: Courtesy Library of Congress p. 16: Top
Right: Courtesy Library of Congress p. 16: Bottom
Left: Courtesy Library of Congress p. 17: Top Left:
Courtesy Library of Congress p. 17: Top Right:
Courtesy Library of Congress p. 17: Bottom:
Interim Archives/Getty Images pp. 18–19:
Hulton Archive/Getty Images p. 19: Top Middle:
Universal History Archive/UIG via Getty Images
p. 19: Top Right: Courtesy Library of Congress
p. 19: Bottom Left: Fotosearch/Getty Images p.
19: Bottom Right: Courtesy Library of Congress
p. 20: © North Wind Picture Archives/Alamy p.
21: Top Left: Courtesy Library of Congress p. 21:

Top Right: Courtesy Library of Congress p. 21:
Bottom Left: Time Life Pictures/National Park
Service/Harpers Ferry National Historic Park/
The LIFE Picture Collection/Getty Images p. 21:
Bottom Right: Courtesy Library of Congress p.
22: Left: © Everett Collection Historical / Alamy
p. 22: Right: Courtesy Library of Congress p. 23:
Top Left: Courtesy Library of Congress p. 23:
Top Right: Courtesy Library of Congress p. 23:
Bottom: © Niday Picture Library / Alamy p. 24:
Top Left: Courtesy Library of Congress p. 24:
Top Right: Courtesy Library of Congress p. 24:
Bottom Left: Courtesy Library of Congress p. 24:
Bottom Right: Courtesy Library of Congress p.
25: Top: Buyenlarge/Getty Images p. 25: Middle:
Courtesy Library of Congress p. 25: Bottom:
Kean Collection/Getty Images p. 26: Bottom Left:
Courtesy Library of Congress pp. 26–27: Robert N.
Dennis collection of stereoscopic views. Miriam
and Ira D. Wallach Division of Art, Prints and
Photographs, The New York Public Library, Astor,
Lenox and Tilden Foundations p. 27: Bottom
Right: Stock Montage/Getty Images

2: 1861: BROTHER AGAINST BROTHER
pp. 28–29: Courtesy Library of Congress p. 30:
Top: Courtesy Library of Congress p. 30: Bottom:
© PMAF Collection/Alamy p. 31: Top Left:
Courtesy Library of Congress p. 31: Top Right:
Hulton Archive/Getty Images p. 31: Top Middle
Right: Universal History Archive/UIG via Getty
Images p. 31: Middle Right: Courtesy Library of
Congress p. 31: Bottom Right: Courtesy Library
of Congress p. 32: Mathew B. Brady/Library Of
Congress/The LIFE Images Collection/Getty
Images) p. 33: Top Left: Buyenlarge/Getty Images
p. 33: MPI/Stringer p. 33: Bottom Right: © Don
Troiani/Corbis p. 33: Bottom Left: © Niday
Picture Library / Alamy p. 34: Top: Keystone-
France/Gamma-Keystone via Getty Images
p. 34: Bottom: MPI/Getty Images p. 35: Left:
© Everett Collection Historical / Alamy p. 35:
Right: © Classic Image / Alamy p. 36: © Archive
Images/Alamy p. 37: Top Left: Courtesy Library
of Congress p. 37: Top Right: Courtesy Wikimedia
Commons p. 37: Bottom: Courtesy Library of
Congress p. 38: Top: Courtesy Library of Congress
p. 38: Bottom: Kean Collection/Getty Images
p. 39: Left: Courtesy Library of Congress p. 39:
Right: Courtesy National Archives and Records
Administration p. 40: © North Wind Picture
Archives / Alamy. p. 41: Fotosearch / Stringer p.
42: Archive Photos/Getty Images p. 43: Top Left:
Courtesy Library of Congress p. 43: Top Right:
Courtesy Library of Congress p. 43: Bottom Left:
Courtesy Library of Congress p. 43: Bottom Right:
Courtesy Library of Congress p. 44: © Everett
Collection Historical/Alamy p. 45: Buyenlarge/
Getty Images p. 46: Top: Encyclopaedia Britannica
/ Contributor p. 46: Bottom Left: Courtesy
National Archives and Records Administration
p. 46: Bottom Right: Buyenlarge / Contributor p.
47: Top: Courtesy Library of Congress p. 48: Top:
© Bettmann/CORBIS p. 48: Bottom: Courtesy
National Archives and Records Administration
p. 49: Top: Courtesy Library of Congress p.
49: Bottom Left: © Medford Historical Society
Collection/CORBIS p. 49: Bottom Right: Courtesy
Library of Congress p. 50: Courtesy Library of
Congress p. 51: Top Left: Courtesy Library of
Congress p. 51: Top Right: PhotoQuest/Getty
Images p. 51: Bottom: Courtesy Library of

Congress

3: I HAVE ENTERED THE RANKS
pp. 52–53: Courtesy Library of Congress p. 54:
Buyenlarge/Getty Images p. 55: Top: © PF-
(bygone1)/Alamy p. 55: Middle Left: © Tribune
Content Agency LLC/Alamy p. 55: Middle Right:
Courtesy Library of Congress p. 55: Bottom Left:
Courtesy Library of Congress p. 55: Bottom Right:
Courtesy Library of Congress p. 56: All: Courtesy
Library of Congress p. 57: All: Courtesy Library
of Congress p. 58: Top Left: MPI/Getty Images p.
58: Top Right: Archive Photos/Getty Images p. 58:
Middle: Buyenlarge/Getty Images p. 58: Bottom:
MPI/Getty Images p. 59: Top Left: Courtesy
Library of Congress p. 59: Top Right: Courtesy
Library of Congress p. 59: Middle Right: Mansell/
The LIFE Picture Collection/Getty Images p. 59:
Bottom Left: Alexander Gardner/Buyenlarge/
Getty Images p. 59: Bottom Right: Courtesy
Library of Congress p. 60: Courtesy Library of
Congress p. 61: All: Courtesy Library of Congress
p. 62: Mathew Brady/Henry Guttmann/Getty
Images p. 62: Bottom Left: Courtesy Library
of Congress p. 62: Bottom Middle: Courtesy
Library of Congress p. 62: Bottom Right: Courtesy
Library of Congress p. 63: Top: Buyenlarge/
Getty Images p. 63: Middle: George Barnard/
Buyenlarge/Getty Images p. 63: Bottom Left:
Courtesy Library of Congress p. 63: Bottom Right:
SSPL/Getty Images p. 64: SSPL/Getty Images
p. 65: Top Right: Courtesy Library of Congress
p. 65: Top Right: Courtesy private collection of
Rod Gragg p. 65: Bottom Left: © CORBIS p. 65:
Bottom Right: Courtesy Library of Congress
p. 66: Top Left: Fotosearch/Getty Images Top
Right: © Minnesota Historical Society/CORBIS
p. 66: Middle: MPI/Getty Images p. 66: Bottom:
© Bettmann/CORBIS p. 67: Top Left: © Medford
Historical Society Collection/CORBIS p. 67:
Top Right: Courtesy Library of Congress p. 67:
Bottom Left: © CORBIS p. 67: Bottom Right:
Popperfoto/Getty Images p. 68: Top: Courtesy
Wikimedia Commons p. 68: Bottom: Archive
Photos/Getty Images p. 69: Top Left: Courtesy
Library of Congress p. 69: Top Right: Courtesy
National Archives and Records Administration
p. 69: Middle: © Niday Picture Library/Alamy
p. 69: Bottom Left: Courtesy Library of Congress
p. 69: Bottom Right: Buyenlarge/Getty Images
pp. 70–71: Buyenlarge/Getty Images p. 70:
Bottom Left: Courtesy Library of Congress p. 70:
Bottom Right: Courtesy Library of Congress p.
70–71: Bottom Right: Alexander Gardner/MPI/
Getty Images pp. 72–73: Top Left: Buyenlarge/
Getty Images p. 73: Top Right: Courtesy AP Photo
p. 73: Bottom Left: Courtesy Library of Congress
p. 73: Bottom Right: Courtesy Library of Congress
p. 74: Top: Courtesy Library of Congress p. 74:
Middle Left: Courtesy Library of Congress p. 74:
Middle Right: Mathew Brady/Kean Collection/
Getty Images p. 74: Bottom: Courtesy Library
of Congress p. 75: Top Left: Courtesy Library of
Congress p. 75: Top Middle: Courtesy Library
of Congress p. 75: Top Right: © CORBIS p. 75:
Middle: Archive Photos/Getty Images p. 75:
Bottom Left: Archive Photos/Getty Images p.
75: Bottom Right: Hulton Archive/Getty Images
p. 76: © Medford Historical Society Collection/
CORBIS p. 77: Top Left: © Bettmann/CORBIS/AP
Images p. 77: Top Right: © CORBIS p. 77: Middle
Left: Buyenlarge/Getty Images p. 77: Bottom

Left: Courtesy Library of Congress p. 77: Bottom Middle: Courtesy Library of Congress p. 77: Bottom Right: Courtesy Library of Congress p. 78: Top: MPI/Getty Images p. 78: Bottom: Kean Collection/Archive Photos/Getty Images p. 79: Top: Courtesy National Archives & Records Association p. 79: Bottom: Buyenlarge/Getty Images p. 80: Top Left: Courtesy Library of Congress p. 80: Top Right: Courtesy Library of Congress p. 80: Middle: Alexander Gardner/Buyenlarge/Getty Images p. 80: Bottom: George N. Barnard/Buyenlarge/Getty Images p. 81: Top Left: Courtesy Library of Congress p. 81: Top Right: Courtesy Library of Congress p. 81: Bottom Left: George S. Cook/Buyenlarge/Getty Images p. 81: Bottom Right: Courtesy Library of Congress p. 82: All: Courtesy Library of Congress p. 83: Top Left: © Tribune Content Agency LLC/Alamy 83: Top Right: Courtesy Library of Congress p. 83: Middle Right: Courtesy Library of Congress p. 83: Bottom Left: Courtesy Library of Congress p. 83: Bottom Middle: Courtesy National Archives & Records Association p. 83: Bottom Right: Courtesy Library of Congress

4: 1862: A COUNTRY TORN ASUNDER
pp. 84–85: Courtesy Library of Congress p. 86: Left: Hulton Archive/Getty Images p. 86: Right: Courtesy Library of Congress p. 87: Top Left: Kean Collection/Getty Images p. 87: Top Right: Courtesy Library of Congress p. 87: Middle Right: Courtesy Library of Congress: Courtesy Library of Congress p. 87: Bottom Right: Courtesy Library of Congress p. 88: Top Right: Courtesy Library of Congress p. 88: Bottom Left: Courtesy Library of Congress p. 89: Courtesy Library of Congress p. 90: Courtesy Library of Congress p. 91: Top Left: © CORBIS p. 91: Top Right: © Ivy Close Images/Alamy p. 91: Bottom Left: © CORBIS p. 91: Bottom Right: Courtesy Library of Congress p. 92: Universal History Archive/Getty Images p. 93: Top: © CORBIS p. 93: Bottom: © Ivy Close Images/Alamy p. 94: Top: Buyenlarge/Getty Images p. 94: Bottom Left: Courtesy Library of Congress p. 95: Top Left: Courtesy National Archives and Records p. 95: Top Right: Courtesy Library of Congress p. 95: Bottom: © CORBIS p. 96–97: Top Left: Kean Collection/Getty Images p. 97: Top Right: Courtesy Library of Congress p. 97: Bottom: Interim Archives/Getty Images p. 98: © CORBIS p. 99: Top Left: Matthew Brady/MPI/Getty Images p. 99: Top Right: Courtesy Library of Congress p. 99: Middle Left: Otto Herschan/Getty Images p. 99: Bottom Left: Courtesy Library of Congress p. 99: Bottom Right: © Medford Historical Society Collection/CORBIS p. 100: Top Left: Courtesy Library of Congress pp. 100–101: Matthew Brady/Buyenlarge/Getty Images p. 101: Bottom Left: MPI/Getty Images p. 101: Bottom Right: © CORBIS p. 102: Kean Collection/Archive Photos/Getty Images p. 103: Top Left: Courtesy Library of Congress p. 103: Top Right: Courtesy Library of Congress p. 103: Middle Right: © CORBIS p. 103: Bottom Left: Courtesy Library of Congress p. 103: Bottom Right: © Medford Historical Society Collection/CORBIS p. 104: Top: Courtesy Library of Congress p. 104: Bottom: Courtesy Library of Congress p. 105: Top: Courtesy Library of Congress p. 105: Bottom: Courtesy Library of Congress p. 106: Courtesy Library of Congress p.

107: Top Left: © Niday Picture Library/Alamy p. 107: Top Right: © Niday Picture Library/Alamy p. 107: Bottom: Courtesy Library of Congress p. 108: © CORBIS p. 109: Left: Courtesy Library of Congress p. 109: Top Right: Buyenlarge/Getty Images p. 109: Bottom Right: Buyenlarge/Getty Images p. 110: © Bettmann/CORBIS p. 111: Top: © CORBIS p. 111: Bottom Left: Courtesy Library of Congress p. 111: Bottom Right: Courtesy National Archives & Records Association p. 112: Top Left: : Courtesy National Archives & Records Association p. 112: Top Right: Everett Collection Inc/Alamy p. 113: Top: Courtesy Library of Congress p. 113: Bottom: Courtesy Library of Congress pp. 114–115: Left: © Stocktrek Images, Inc./Alamy p. 115: Right: AP Photo/Library of Congress p. 116: Top: © CSU Archives/Everett Collection Historical/Alamy p. 116: Bottom: Alexander Gardner/Buyenlarge/Getty Images p. 118: Top: Courtesy Library of Congress p. 118: Bottom Left: Courtesy Library of Congress p. 119: Top: Courtesy Library of Congress p. 119: Bottom: Courtesy National Park Service p. 120: Top: Courtesy Library of Congress p. 120: Bottom: Courtesy Library of Congress p. 121: Top: Courtesy Library of Congress p. 121: Middle: Kean Collection/Archive Photos/Getty Images p. 121: Bottom: Courtesy Library of Congress

5: THE WAR ON WATER
pp. 122–123: Lindy Powers/Getty Images p. 124: Buyenlarge/Getty Images p. 125: Top: Courtesy U.S. Naval History & Heritage Command p. 125: Top Right: © CORBIS p. 125: Middle Right: © CORBIS p. 125: Bottom Left: Lindy Powers/Getty Images p. 125: Bottom Right: © Medford Historical Society Collection/CORBIS p. 126: © ClassicStock/Alamy p. 127: Top Left: © North Wind Picture Archives/Alamy p. 127: Top Right: © Ivy Close Images/Alamy p. 127: Interim Archive/Getty Images p. 128: Top: Courtesy Library of Congress p. 128: Bottom: Courtesy Library of Congress p. 129: Top: © CORBIS p. 129: Middle Left: © CORBIS p. 129: Middle Right: Courtesy Library of Congress p. 129: Bottom: Archive Photos/Getty Images p. 129: Bottom Right: MPI/Getty Images p. 130: Top Left: Courtesy Library of Congress p. 130: Bottom Left: © The Mariners' Museum/CORBIS p. 130: Bottom Right: © The Mariners' Museum/CORBIS p. 131: Top: Courtesy US Naval History & Heritage Command p. 131: Bottom: Buyenlarge/Getty Images p. 132: © CORBIS p. 133: Top: Courtesy National Archives & Records Association p. 133: Bottom Left: Courtesy US Naval History & Heritage Command p. 133: Bottom Right: Buyenlarge/Getty Images p. 134: © CORBIS p. 135: Top Left: Buyenlarge/Getty Images p. 135: Top Right: © Medford Historical Society Collection/CORBIS p. 135: Middle: © Medford Historical Society Collection/CORBIS p. 135: Bottom Left: © CORBIS p. 135: Bottom Right: © CORBIS pp. 136–137: Bottom Left: Courtesy Library of Congress p. 137: Top: Courtesy Library of Congress p. 137: Bottom Right: © Granamour Weems Collection/Alamy p. 138–139: Left: 3LH-Fine Art/Getty Images p. 139: Right: Courtesy Library of Congress pp. 140–141: Top: Courtesy US Naval History & Heritage Command p. 140: Bottom: Courtesy US Naval History & Heritage Command p. 141: Bottom

Left: Fotosearch/Getty Images p. 141: Courtesy US Naval History & Heritage Command pp. 142–143: Left: © Archive Images/Alamy p. 143: Right: © Medford Historical Society Collection/CORBIS p. 144: Top Left: Fotosearch/Getty Images p. 144: Top Right: © Mary Evans Picture Library/Alamy p. 144: Bottom: John Parrot/Stocktrek Images/Getty Images p. 145: Top: © Bettmann/CORBIS p. 145: Bottom Left: Courtesy Library of Congress p. 145: Bottom Right: Buyenlarge/Getty Images pp. 146–147: Top Left: Courtesy Library of Congress p. 147: Top Right: Courtesy Library of Congress p. 147: Middle: Courtesy Library of Congress p. 147: Bottom: Courtesy Library of Congress p. 148: Top Left: Courtesy Library of Congress p. 148: Top Right: Buyenlarge/Getty Images p. 149: Top: Courtesy Library of Congress p. 149: Bottom Left: © ClassicStock/Alamy p. 149: Bottom Right: Courtesy US Navel History & Heritage Command

6: 1863: THE TURNING POINT
pp. 150–151: Tetra Images/Getty Images pp. 152–153: Hulton Archive/Getty Images p. 154: Time Life Pictures/National Archives/The LIFE Picture Collection/Getty Images p. 155: Top Left: Courtesy Library of Congress p. 155: Top Right: Courtesy Library of Congress p. 155: Upper Middle Right: Courtesy Library of Congress p. 155: Bottom Left: © Everett Collection Historical/Alamy p. 155: Middle Bottom Right: Courtesy Library of Congress 155: Bottom Right: Courtesy Library of Congress p. 156: Kean Collection/Archive Photos/Getty Images p. 157: Top: Courtesy Library of Congress p. 157: Bottom Left: Courtesy Library of Congress p. 157: Bottom Middle: Courtesy Library of Congress p. 157: Bottom Right: Courtesy Library of Congress p. 158: Courtesy Library of Congress p. 159: Top Left: Courtesy Library of Congress p. 159: Top Right: Courtesy Library of Congress p. 159: Bottom: Courtesy Library of Congress p. 160: Courtesy Library of Congress p. 161: Top: Courtesy Library of Congress p. 161: Bottom Left: Buyenlarge/Getty Images p. 161: Bottom Right: Courtesy Library of Congress p. 162: A J Russell/Getty Images p. 163: Top Left: Courtesy National Archives & Records Association p. 163: Top Right: Courtesy National Archives & Records Association p. 163: Bottom Left: Courtesy National Archives & Records Association p. 163: Bottom Right: The Print Collector/Print Collector/Getty Images p. 164: Courtesy Library of Congress p. 165: Top: Buyenlarge/Getty Images p. 165: Bottom Left: Courtesy Library of Congress p. 165: Bottom Right: Courtesy Library of Congress pp. 166–167: Courtesy Library of Congress p. 168: Top: Courtesy National Archives & Records Association p. 168: Bottom: Courtesy Library of Congress p. 169: Left: MPI/Getty Images p. 169: Top Right: Courtesy Library of Congress p. 169: Bottom Right: Courtesy Library of Congress p. 170: Top: Courtesy Library of Congress p. 170: Bottom: Courtesy Library of Congress p. 171: Top: Courtesy Library of Congress p. 171: Bottom: Archive Photos/Getty Images p. 172: Top Right: Courtesy Library of Congress p. 172: Bottom: Courtesy Library of Congress p. 173: Top Left: Courtesy Library of Congress p. 173: Top Right: Courtesy Library of Congress p. 173: Bottom: Courtesy Library of Congress p. 174:

TIME LIFE BOOKS

TIME HOME ENTERTAINMENT

Publisher Margot Schupf
Vice President, Finance Vandana Patel
Executive Director, Marketing Services Carol Pittard
Executive Director, Business Development Suzanne Albert
Executive Director, Marketing Susan Hettleman
Publishing Director Megan Pearlman
Associate Director of Publicity Courtney Greenhalgh
Assistant General Counsel Simone Procas
Assistant Director, Special Sales Ilene Schreider
Assistant Director, Finance Christine Font
Senior Manager, Sales Marketing Danielle Costa
Associate Production Manager Kimberly Marshall
Associate Prepress Manager Alex Voznesenskiy
Associate Project Manager Stephanie Braga

Editorial Director Stephen Koepp
Art Director Gary Stewart
Senior Editors Roe D'Angelo, Alyssa Smith
Managing Editor Matt DeMazza
Project Editor Eileen Daspin
Copy Chief Rina Bander
Design Manager Anne-Michelle Gallero
Assistant Managing Editor Gina Scauzillo
Editorial Assistant Courtney Mifsud

Special thanks: Allyson Angle, Katherine Barnet, Brad Beatson, Jeremy Biloon, John Champlin, Ian Chin, Susan Chodakiewicz, Rose Cirrincione, Assu Etsubneh, Mariana Evans, Alison Foster, Kristina Jutzi, David Kahn, Jean Kennedy, Hillary Leary, Amanda Lipnick, Samantha Long, Amy Mangus, Robert Martells, Nina Mistry, Melissa Presti, Danielle Prielipp, Kate Roncinske, Babette Ross, Dave Rozzelle, Matthew Ryan, Ricardo Santiago, Divyam Shrivastava

Published by Time Home Entertainment Inc.
1271 Avenue of the Americas, 6th floor • New York, NY 10020

ISBN 10: 1-61893-148-2
ISBN 13: 978-1-61893-148-1

We welcome your comments and suggestions about Time Home Entertainment books. Please write to us at:
Time Home Entertainment books, Attention: Book Editors, P.O. Box 361095, Des Moines, IA 50336-1095
If you would like to order any of our hardcover Collector's Edition books, please call us at 800-327-6388, Monday through Friday, 7 a.m.–9 p.m. Central Time.

Produced by becker&mayer! LLC
Writer Rod Gragg